Student Speech Policy Readability
in Public Schools

Erica Salkin • Logan Shenkel

Student Speech Policy Readability in Public Schools

Interpretation, Application, and Elevation of Student Handbook Language

Erica Salkin
Whitworth University
Spokane, Washington, USA

Logan Shenkel
Whitworth University
Spokane, Washington, USA

ISBN 978-3-319-82990-6   ISBN 978-3-319-44132-0 (eBook)
DOI 10.1007/978-3-319-44132-0

Cover illustration: Détail de la Tour Eiffel © nemesis2207/Fotolia.co.uk

Printed on acid-free paper

This Palgrave Macmillan imprint is published by Springer Nature
The registered company is Springer International Publishing AG
The registered company address is: Gewerbestrasse 11, 6330 Cham, Switzerland

ACKNOWLEDGMENTS

We would like to acknowledge and thank the high school teachers who allowed us to visit their classrooms as we pursued this project. Your support for research into student speech policy highlights your commitment to teaching tomorrow's citizens. We are truly grateful.

CONTENTS

LIST OF TABLES

CHAPTER 1

Introduction: Student Handbooks and the First Amendment

Abstract After Briana Popour was asked to go home for wearing a T-shirt to school that read "Nobody knows I'm a lesbian," she argued that the school's speech and dress policies did not prohibit her from wearing the shirt on the school premises. While the First Amendment is black and white in theory, its application appears to be far grayer. Because of the degree of focus and the intentionality toward a student audience, this book explores student speech policy as it is conveyed in student handbooks. It does so specifically by exploring previous Supreme Court cases with regard to student expression, readability metrics, qualitative student application, and external research.

Keywords Free speech · Student handbooks · Student policy · Public schools

In September, 2015, Briana Popour of Chesnee, South Carolina, wore a T-shirt to school that read "Nobody knows I'm a lesbian."[1] Printed in white block letters against dark pink, the shirt not only drew few comments from her fellow students but also did catch the attention of her teachers. She was summoned to the school's main office and told to change her shirt or go home.

Popour was familiar with her school's student handbook, and argued that the school's speech and dress policies did not prohibit her from

© The Author(s) 2017
E. Salkin, L. Shenkel, *Student Speech Policy Readability in Public Schools*, DOI 10.1007/978-3-319-44132-0_1

wearing the T-shirt. The response, as she described to area media outlets, was, "Well, not everything is in the handbook."[2] When reporters followed up with the school, the district responded via e-mail "that the shirt was 'offensive and distracting' and pointed to a section in the dress code that said, 'Clothing deemed distracting, revealing, overly suggestive or otherwise disruptive will not be permitted.' "[3]

Both the student and her mother pushed back against the school's eventual disciplinary action. The core of their dispute was twofold: what does "disruptive" mean, and who gets to make the judgment call that defines it?

These questions are not unique, especially when it comes to public school regulation of student expression. While the First Amendment approach to expression is straightforward on paper—"Congress shall make no law...abridging freedom of speech, or of the press"[4]—the amendment's application is far more complex. Government bodies are challenged to proactively state in "plain language" the speech rights and responsibilities of individuals under their authority, and public schools are no exception. Public K-12 administrators need to balance the needs of the classroom and the orderly educational environment with the constitutional rights of students when they create comprehensive policy protecting rights to free speech within public schools.

Equally important as administrative understanding of public school student speech rights is student understanding of public school student speech rights. That comprehension also brings its own challenges. Public school students can, if they wish, track down the common law approach to student speech, starting with the *Tinker v. Des Moines Independent Community School District*[5] decision of 1969. Reading and understanding Supreme Court cases, however, can be difficult for young people without guidance. Students can, if they wish, consult the hundreds of excellent books, high-quality journal articles, and extraordinary websites that discuss student speech rights in public schools for direction regarding the breadth and depth of those rights. Such a desire to learn would need to be accompanied by intense motivation, however, and even such highly motivated students may become confused or discouraged in their search, as they will continually encounter a regular caution to refer to one's own school district for the most relevant guidance.

For the most highly motivated student, then, the path lies in their own school district policies, generally created by locally elected school boards in accordance with state education law or policy. These policies are written by adults and often for adults, such as parents, building administrators, teachers, and community members. They spell out the rules and responsibilities of all parties involved in the K-12 experience and must comply with all applicable legal authorities, from the U.S. Constitution to area municipal ordinances. As such, district policies are heavily influenced by legal language that can make for tough reading. While "ignorance of the law is no excuse for breaking it," an incomprehensible, wordy, or convoluted law or policy is difficult to obey.

This brings us back to Briana Popour and her application of her school's policy to her T-shirt. Popour turned to her school's student handbook for guidance on the type of expression she could engage in without fear of disciplinary action, and was still confounded when she attempted to apply the policy because of its lack of clarity. Popour's situation highlights the principle that to adequately serve the students who are bound by district policies on issues such as student expression, those policies must be understandable to the students themselves.

There are two approaches we could take to better understand how students interpret and use school district policies created to address student expression. We could focus on student engagement with district policies. We know students have easy access to district or school board policies; as in most cases, these policies are available on district websites. Despite this easy access, exploring student interactions with district/board policies is not an ideal place to start. Such policies are written for a broad and, primarily, adult audience, and not crafted specifically for a student audience to read and use. It would be too easy to attribute any perceived lack of comprehension to the wordiness or complexity that comes from crafting rules that must comply with local, state, and federal laws.

A second approach, then, uses a presentation of student speech/expression policy that is included in a document designed specifically for students: student handbooks. Many states mandate the creation and annual distribution of student handbooks to ensure that students are familiar with the policies that guide their conduct during the school day. These documents are created intentionally for a student audience, and as such, are an ideal opportunity to explore how and with what degree of success student expression rights are communicated to public school students. Because of that degree of focus and intentionality toward a student audience, this project explores student speech policy as it is conveyed in student hand-books with three specific questions in mind:

1) Do handbooks take up the topic of student expression at all?
2) If they do, how "readable" is the presentation of student expression rights and responsibilities? Does that readability correlate with the grade levels of its intended audience?
3) How do students interpret and apply handbook entries on student expression?

Chapter 2 details the current legal approach to student expression in public schools, including four key Supreme Court cases, lower court interpretations, and state statutory approaches. These legal authorities create the foundation for student expression policies and must be reflected in any approach to student speech in a public school.

In chap. 3, we explore the literature on readability and law. Concern about readability of law and policy on essential rights such as privacy, safety, and public education has been the topic of research for more than 50 years. There exists a tension between ensuring that the law or policy says precisely what it must say to remain valid, and phrasing the law or policy in such a way that the average reader can understand and apply it. This tension has increased in the digital age as federal agencies require online platforms to inform users of their rights when they engage with tools that collect personal data.

Readability metrics can guide us on the fit between the language and its audience, and in chap. 5, we apply common readability calculators to a randomly selected collection of student handbooks to see if sections on student expression are written for the student audiences they are meant to serve. Those metrics are compared to an identical analysis on student hand-book sections devoted to student dress to create a point of comparison, and all sections are also analyzed qualitatively for key themes and construction. For a second point of comparison, an additional analysis is presented on a selection of student handbooks from private schools to examine the possi-bility that public schools' mandate to comply with the First Amendment impacts readability, construction, or content of expression policies.

Readability is largely hypothetical, however, and thus in chap. 6 we put student handbook language on student expression in front of public high school students and ask for their interpretations and applications. Through a series of focus groups, we see the social and cultural meanings that students attach to the language of student expression policy and the challenges they have with finding the line between protected and unprotected speech while on campus. Their feedback helps highlight the idea that speech isn't just a legal concern, but also a cultural and social one. Students expect their speech and expression policies to reflect those elements as well.

Finally, we conclude with a discussion of application of these findings. How can schools use this information to create more comprehensive, student-friendly policies on student expression that comply with the law, protect the effective learning environment, and inform their student audiences?

Student expression can offer a valuable asset to the learning experience—many studies have affirmed that public school students who have the opportunity to engage with principles of free speech or press are more interested in civic life, more willing to get involved in community initiatives, and more likely to feel they have the ability to make real and lasting change in their worlds.[6] Uncertainty about the level of speech protection they have, however, creates a chilling effect—research supports the assertion that students will back away from engaging in expression rather than risk disciplinary actions when the line between protected and unprotected is unclear.[7] This vagueness robs students of the learning opportunities inherent in expression—clarity in student handbook language surrounding student expression rights can remove the "chill" and allow students to enjoy their constitutional right to expression as it is conceived in the public school environment with confidence.

NOTES

1. Addie Hampton, "Chesnee HS Student Questioning Suspension For "Lesbian" Shirt," WSPA.com, September 9, 2015.
2. *Id.*
3. Tierney Sneed, "S.C. High School Student Suspended for 'Nobody Knows I'm A Lesbian' T-Shirt," TalkingPointsMemo.com, September 11, 2015.
4. U.S. Constitution, Amendment I.
5. 393 U.S. 503 (1969).
6. See, for example, P.S. Bobkowski & P.R. Miller. "Civic implications of secondary school journalism: Associations with voting propensity and community volunteering," *Journalism and Mass Communication Quarterly*, published online before print doi: 10.1177/1077699016628821 (2016).
7. Matt Wynn. "Threat of censorship has 'chilling effect.'" *Quill* 90, no. 3 (2002): 40.

REFERENCES

Bobkowski, P. S., & Miller, P. R., "Civic implications of secondary school journalism: Associations with voting propensity and community volunteering," *Journalism and Mass Communication Quarterly*, published online before print doi: 10.1177/1077699016628821 (2016).

Hampton, Addie Hampton. "Chesnee HS Student Questioning Suspension For "Lesbian" Shirt," *WSPA.com*, September 9, 2015.

Sneed, Tierney. "S.C. High School Student Suspended for 'Nobody Knows I'm A Lesbian' T-Shirt," *TalkingPointsMemo.com*, September 11, 2015.

Tinker v. Des Moines Independent Community School District, 393 U.S. 503 (1969).

U.S. Constitution, Amendment. I.

Wynn, M., "Threat of censorship has 'chilling effect.' " *Quill 90*, no. 3 (2002): 40.

The Supreme Court and Student Speech

Abstract The U.S. Supreme Court has, over the course of the past 50 years, created guidelines for student expression within the public school system. Salkin and Shenkel depict the four key Supreme Court cases that formed these guidelines: *Tinker v. Des Moines Independent Community School District, Bethel School District v. Fraser, Hazelwood v. Kuhlmeier,* and *Morse v. Frederick.* As a result of these precedents, student speech that is related to illegal drug use can be regulated per *Morse,* speech that is lewd or vulgar can be regulated per *Fraser,* speech that is reasonably seen as school-sponsored can be regulated per *Hazelwood,* and all other student speech regulation is assessed by the *Tinker* standard, which allows regulation only for student speech that materially disrupts the academic environment.

Keywords Tinker · Fraser · Hazelwood · Morse · Cyberspeech

Student speech rights in public schools[1] are largely defined by four key Supreme Court cases spanning nearly 40 years. These cases form the backbone of student speech policy, as they outline the specifics of students' rights to free speech and expression within the public school environment.

© The Author(s) 2017
E. Salkin, L. Shenkel, *Student Speech Policy Readability in Public Schools,* DOI 10.1007/978-3-319-44132-0_2

In, 1969, the Supreme Court heard *Tinker v. Des Moines Independent Community School District*,[2] in which three public school students contested the suspension they received for wearing black armbands marked with peace symbols to school. The students—Mary Beth and John Tinker along with Christopher Eckhardt—wore the armbands in silent protest to the Vietnam War, and were told by school officials that they were forbidden from returning to school until they chose to remove the armbands.[3] Instead, the families took the school district to court.

When the case eventually reached the U.S. Supreme Court, the justices, in a 7–2 decision, determined that the school's actions were an unconstitutional infringement of the students' right to free speech. Writing for the majority, Justice Abe Fortas wrote:

> First Amendment rights, applied in light of the special characteristics of the school environment, are available to teachers and students. It can hardly be argued that either students or teachers shed their constitutional rights to freedom of speech or expression at the schoolhouse gate.[4]

Fortas noted that constitutionally protected speech may appear to be a "hazardous freedom"[5] in any environment, but fear or apprehension of ideas can't support the regulation of expression. Instead, school regulations of student speech could only be upheld if such speech "would substantially interfere with the work of the school or impinge upon the rights of other students."[6]

The Court did clarify that the armbands at the heart of *Tinker* were a form of "pure speech," with clear expressive intent and likelihood of understanding. This recognition separated the Tinkers' act of expression from an action that might be done to share a message, but isn't always clearly understood, such as choices in clothing or hairstyles.[7] While later cases such as *Spence v. Washington*[8] and *Texas v. Johnson*[9] clarified definitions of expressive conduct that could roll clothing and hairstyle choice into considerations of First Amendment rights, in 1969, the clear protest intent behind the armbands elevated them to a more intentional and understood form of expression in the Court's eyes.

The post-*Tinker* era saw an upsurge of court cases involving student speech rights as part of an overall increase in legal activity about the constitutional rights of children. The 1960s and 1970s were, among other things, noted for the children's movement, and while young people and their parents sought to figure out how fundamental freedoms applies to minors, they also explored how such rights applied to public school students.[10] Outcomes were not uniform, as courts showed a clear deference to administrators and educators on the evaluation of the both a "material disruption" and the likelihood of its occurrence.

The U.S. Supreme Court did not revisit student speech concerns again until 1986 with *Bethel School District v. Fraser*.[11] Matthew Fraser was suspended for delivering a sexually suggestive speech nominating a friend for student government during a school assembly:

> I know a man who is firm—he's firm in his pants, he's firm in his shirt, his character is firm—but most . . . of all, his belief in you, the students of Bethel, is firm. Jeff Kuhlman is a man who takes his point and pounds it in. If necessary, he'll take an issue and nail it to the wall. He doesn't attack things in spurts—he drives hard, pushing and pushing until finally—he succeeds. Jeff is a man who will go to the very end—even the climax, for each and every one of you. So vote for Jeff for A.S.B. vice-president—he'll never come between you and the best our high school can be.[12]

The school argued that Fraser's speech violated a school rule prohibiting speech that "materially and substantially interferes with the educational process is prohibited, including the use of obscene, profane language or gestures."[13] Fraser sued, claiming the school failed to show his speech caused such an interference. The federal district and circuit courts, applying the *Tinker* standard, agreed with Fraser.[14]

The Supreme Court reversed, affirming the school's disciplinary decisions and stating that the constitutional protection of free speech "does not prevent the school officials from determining that to permit a vulgar and lewd speech such as respondent's would undermine the school's basic educational mission."[15] Noting that schools are tasked with both educating and socializing the students under their care, Chief Justice Warren Burger differentiated Fraser's speech from the political message at the heart of the *Tinker* decision, and instead focused on the goal of the school to inculcate the "fundamental values of habits and manners of civility"[16] necessary to a democratic society.

Fraser introduced a categorical approach[17] to the regulation of student speech, which is not too dissimilar from how free speech is evaluated outside of academic environments. The next Supreme Court case involving student speech—*Hazelwood v. Kuhlmeier*[18]—brought forum analysis[19] to the school context. This case dealt with an administrator's decision to remove two pages from the Hazelwood East student newspaper, *Spectrum*, prior to its publication. The administrator had concerns regarding articles on divorce and student pregnancy, believing the articles created a liability risk for libel and invasion of privacy.

The student editors of the *Spectrum* claimed the removal was an infringement of their right to free press. Their suit was eventually heard by the Supreme Court, which acknowledged the relevance of *Tinker* and *Fraser*, but distinguished this situation because of the particular forum (or platform) in which this speech occurred—a student newspaper created in a classroom and partially funded by the school. In the Court's analysis, the newspaper's strong connection to the school, as evidenced by the facts that it was produced in a class, the students responsible for its production received credit and grades for their efforts, and the actions of the newspaper staff as a whole were directly overseen by a teacher, transformed the newspaper from an independent student voice to a government-regulated forum. The Court noted the intention behind the newspaper appeared to be to promote a learning experience rather than create a broad opportunity for students or the public to voice a wide range of ideas or opinions. As such, the Court deemed the newspaper to be open to regulation "in any reasonable manner."[20]

The *Hazelwood* precedent of reasonable manner regulation covers "student speech in school-sponsored expressive activities,"[21] meaning any expressive activity occurring within that school-sponsored forum (such as newspapers, yearbooks,[22] theatrical performances,[23] and any classroom[24] including teacher speech[25]) need only meet what's known as the "rational basis" test to defend against a free speech claim. In an academic setting, the Court defined "rational basis" as a "legitimate pedagogical purpose."[26] In other words, schools can regulate student speech when it occurs in a school-sponsored environment, like a school-sponsored newspaper, yearbook, or other expressive activity, if the reason for the regulation is tied to the learning experience itself. In the case of *Hazelwood*, the school was able to prove that the regulation was supported by the newspaper class's learning goals of quality journalism that complied with the law. The Court noted, however, that schools could not regulate school-sponsored speech merely because administrators disagreed with the students' perspectives or opinions.

The latest exploration of student speech rights in public schools came through *Morse v. Frederick*.[27] High school senior Joseph Frederick skipped school the morning that all students were attending a public event to witness the journey of the Olympic torch through downtown Juneau, Alaska. He met up with friends prior to the torch's passing, however, and when it did, he unfurled a banner reading "BONG HiTS 4 JESUS." Frederick himself admitted that the banner was a nonsensical phrase meant to attract attention of attending media, but his principal, Deborah Morse, believed it shared an implicit pro-drug message and suspended him when he refused to take it down.[28]

The Supreme Court upheld Morse's actions and denied Frederick's claim that his First Amendment rights had been violated. Chief Justice John Roberts, writing for the majority, argued that schools were not required to tolerate student expression that contributes to the social or physical dangers that schools are charged to prevent, and illegal drug use is a clear and powerful concern for American schools.[29] While the Court was not willing to go as far as deeming the speech open to regulation because it was "offensive" (a highly subjective term[30]), it did believe that speech reasonably viewed as promoting illegal drug use was clearly open to school regulation and punishment.

As a result of these four Supreme Court precedents, student speech that is related to illegal drug use can be regulated per *Morse*, speech that is lewd or vulgar can be regulated per *Fraser*, speech that is reasonably seen as school-sponsored can be regulated per *Hazelwood*, and all other student speech regulation is assessed by the *Tinker* standard.

Lower courts have worked to apply these precedents to modern student speech concerns; most notably, to issues involving cyberspeech. All four precedents occurred at a time when the student and the speech were both clearly within school authority—on school grounds, during the school day, or during a school-sponsored activity.[31] Online speech, especially through social media, occurs at all times and from all places, but the impact of such speech easily ripples into the academic environment. As schools have sought to address the effects of cyberspeech on the classroom, they have struggled to determine the reach of their authority while honoring the First Amendment.

Lower courts have adopted three different approaches to assessing the ability of public schools to regulate student cyberspeech that does not originate during the school day or on school grounds. A California federal district court summed up these approaches as follows:

First, the majority of courts will apply *Tinker* where speech originating off campus is brought to school or to the attention of school authorities, whether by the author himself or some other means. The end result established by these cases is that any speech, regardless of its geographic origin, which causes or is foreseeably likely to cause a substantial disruption of school activities can be regulated by the school.

Second, some courts will apply the Supreme Court's student speech precedents, including *Tinker*, only where there is a sufficient nexus between the off-campus speech and the school. It is unclear, however, when such a nexus exists. The Second Circuit has held that a sufficient nexus exists where it is "reasonably foreseeable" that the speech would reach campus. The mere fact that the speech was brought on campus may or may not be sufficient.

Third, in unique cases where the speaker took specific efforts to keep the speech off campus, or clearly did not intend the speech to reach campus and publicized it in such a manner that it was unlikely to do so, the student speech precedents likely should not apply. In these latter scenarios, school officials have no authority, beyond the general principles governing speech in a public arena, to regulate such speech.[32]

What these approaches suggest is when student speech intersects with schools, whether it is physically seen on campus or can reasonably be predicted to ripple into the school environment (through student sharing, discussion, or gossip), it can be regulated or disciplined by school administrators. The California court did, however, struggle with the concept of defining a "sufficient nexus," as such a term relies on a highly subjective foreseeability standard. The "nexus" in *Morse* was clear—even though Morse had skipped school that morning, his decision to stand with his fellow students during the torch run effectively connected his speech to his school. The lack of a physical presence in cyberspeech makes the definition of nexus more challenging. While the court did note some student online speech should not fall under the special speech regulation abilities of public schools, the hands-off approach has only been adopted in a small handful of cases.

In response to the limitations of the *Fraser, Hazelwood,* and *Morse* precedents, 12 states[33] have created statutory or administrative law to ensure freedom of speech and press for public school students. Thanks to the *Gitlow*[34] decision of 1925, state laws must comply with the federal First Amendment protections for speech and expression, but this requirement does not mean states can't create laws that give *more* speech freedom to its citizens. Arkansas,[35] Colorado,[36] Illinois, Iowa,[37] Kansas,[38]

Maryland,[39] Massachusetts,[40] North Dakota,[41] Oregon,[42] Pennsylvania,[43] and Washington[44] each have created law or policy to protect K-12 public school student speech in their states. California is the leader in this initiative, creating two of its five state laws addressing student speech in 1972. California's laws also provide the broadest protections, applying to public community colleges,[45] public secondary schools (including charter schools),[46] public colleges and universities,[47] private secondary schools,[48] and private colleges and universities.[49]

While the laws and rules in these 12 states differ in their exact language, in general, they codify the *Tinker* declaration of student speech rights past the "schoolhouse gate" when such speech does not materially and substantially impact the academic environment. Further, they often clarify in more specific terms when schools are empowered to restrict or regulate. For example, Iowa Code §280.22(2) states:

> Students shall not express, publish, or distribute any of the following:
>
> a. Materials which are obscene.
> b. Materials which are libelous or slanderous under chapter 659.
> c. Materials which encourage students to do any of the following:
>   (1) Commit unlawful acts.
>   (2) Violate lawful school regulations.
>   (3) Cause the material and substantial disruption of the orderly operation of the school.

Many of the other statutes and policies adopt a similar language, affirming a general protection of student expression and publication except in situations in which expression and publication do not generally enjoy First Amendment protection outside of the school environment—such as libel, obscenity, or incitement—and in situations as defined by *Tinker* that cause significant disruption to the work of the school.

The overarching takeaway that this legal overview provides is the idea that student speech can be regulated when such speech threatens the fundamental purpose of the school—to educate—but not when it encroaches on particular opinions or perspectives of people within the school. Student speech regulation also embraces a categorical approach, and those categories are roughly parallel to those created for general environments to regulate lewd/sexual speech, advocacy of criminal activity, or speech that occurs on government property. At its heart, however, is the assumption that students have a constitutional right to free speech unless a government entity can make the compelling argument otherwise—"free" is the default value. The next step is to convey that assumption, and its exceptions, to the students themselves.

NOTES

1. As an extension of government, public schools are considered government actors and therefore are subject to the dictates of the First Amendment, where private schools are not.
2. 393 U.S. 503 (1969)
3. *Id.* at 504.
4. *Id.* at 506.
5. *Id.* at 508.
6. *Id.* at 509.
7. *Id.* at 508.
8. 418 U.S. 405, 410–11 (1974), "An intent to convey a particularized message was present, and in the surrounding circumstances the likelihood was great that the message would be understood by those who viewed it."
9. 491 U.S. 397 (1989). "In deciding whether particular conduct possesses sufficient communicative elements to bring the First Amendment into play, we have asked whether an intent to convey a particularized message was present, and whether the likelihood was great that the message would be understood by those who viewed it." (internal citations omitted)
10. Bruce C. Hafen. *Developing Student Expression Through Institutional Authority: Public Schools as Mediating Structures, Ohio State Law Journal* 48 (1987): 681–86.
11. 478 U.S. 675 (1986).
12. *Id.* at 687 (Brennan, J., concurring)
13. *Id.* at 678.
14. Fraser v. Bethel School District No 403, 755 F.2d 1356 (9th Cir. 1985), Fraser v. Bethel School Dist., No. C83-306T (W.D. Wash. June 8, 1983).
15. *Fraser* 478 U.S. at 685.
16. *Id.* at 681.
17. Categorical approaches match speech to defined categories of speech that have been partially or fully removed from First Amendment protection, such as obscenity or true threats.
18. 484 U.S. 260 (1988).
19. Forum analysis identifies the ability of government to regulate expression occurring in government-regulated "spaces" based on the access granted to

the public. The more accessible a space is, the more difficult it is for government regulation to succeed First Amendment challenge. *See e.g.* International Society for Krishna Consciousness v. Lee, 505 U.S. 672 (1992).

20. *Hazelwood* 484 U.S. at 270.
21. *Id.* at 272–73.
22. *See e.g.* Kincaid v. Gibson, 236 F. 3d 342 (6th Cir. 2001).
23. *See e.g.* Boring v. Buncombe Bd. of Educ., 136 F.3d 364 (4th Cir. 1998).
24. *See e.g.* Miles v. Denver Public Schools, 944 F.2d 773 (10th Cir. 1991).
25. *See e.g.* Bishop v. Aranov, 926 F.2d 1066 (11th Cir. 1991).
26. *Hazelwood* 484 U.S. at 272–73.
27. 551 U.S. 393 (2007).
28. *Id.* at 401.
29. *Id.* at 409–410.
30. *Id.* at 408.
31. There was some disagreement in *Morse v. Frederick* about this element, as Frederick had skipped school on the day of the field trip to watch the torch run through downtown Juneau, but met up with his classmates later to unfurl his controversial banner. The Court did not see this as dispositive, however, stating that Frederick's decision to stand with other students during a school event effectively put him under the authority of the school.
32. J.C. ex rel. R.C. v. Beverly Hills Unified School, 711 F. Supp. 2d 1094, 1107 (C.D. Cal. 2010). This case dealt with the suspension of a student for posting a short video on YouTube of an off-campus conversation she had with friends discussing their mutual dislike of another student at the school. The video upset the named student, who brought it to the attention of the school.
33. As of this writing, several more states have student speech/press statutes working through their legislatures.
34. 268 U.S. 652 (1925).
35. Arkansas Student Publications Act, *Ark. Stat. Ann. Secs. 6–18-1201–1204* (1995).
36. Colorado Student Free Expression Law, *Colo. Rev. Stat. Sec. 22–1-120* (1990).
37. Iowa Student Free Expression Law, *Iowa Code Sec. 280.22* (1989).
38. Kansas Student Publications Act, *Kan. Stat. Ann. Sections 72.1504–72.1506* (1992).
39. Senate Bill 764, signed into law by Governor Larry Hogan on 4/26/16. This law will take effect 10/1/16.
40. Massachusetts Student Free Expression Law, *Mass. Gen. Laws Ann. ch. 71, Section 82* (1988).
41. Student journalists-Freedom of expression, *N.D. Cent. Code §15–10* (2015)

42. Oregon Student Free Expression Law (Public College and Universities), *Ore. Rev. Stat. sec. 351.649* (2007), Oregon Student Free Expression Law (Public Secondary Schools), *Ore. Rev. Stat. sec. 336.477* (2007).
43. Pennsylvania Administrative Code: Student Rights and Responsibilities, *22 Pa. Code Section 12.9* (2005).
44. Washington Administrative Code: Student Rights, *WAC 392–40-215* (1977).
45. California Community College Free Expression Law, *Calif. Educ. Code Section 7612* (1977).
46. California Student Free Expression Law, *Cal. Educ. Code Sec. 48907* (1977).
47. California Leonard Law, *Calif. Educ. Code Section 66301* (2006).
48. California Leonard Law, *Calif. Educ. Code Section 48950* (1992).
49. California Leonard Law, *Calif. Educ. Code Section 94367* (1992).

References

Arkansas Student Publications Act, *Ark. Stat. Ann. Secs. 6-18-1201 – 1204* (1995)
Bethel School District v. Fraser 478 U.S. 675 (1986)
Bishop v. Aranov, 926 F.2d 1066 (11th Cir. 1991)
Boring v. Buncombe Bd. of Educ., 136 F.3d 364 (4th Cir. 1998)
California Community College Free Expression Law, *Calif. Educ. Code Section 7612* (1977)
California Leonard Law, *Calif. Educ. Code Section 48950* (1992)
California Leonard Law, *Calif. Educ. Code Section 66301* (2006)
California Leonard Law, *Calif. Educ. Code Section 94367* (1992)
California Student Free Expression Law, *Cal. Educ. Code Sec. 48907* (1977)
Colorado Student Free Expression Law, *Colo. Rev. Stat. Sec. 22-1-120* (1990)
Fraser v. Bethel School Dist., No. C83-306T (W.D. Wash. June 8, 1983)
Fraser v. Bethel School District No 403, 755 F.2d 1356 (9th Cir. 1985)
Gitlow v. New York 268 U.S. 652 (1925)
Hafen, B. C., "Developing Student Expression Through Institutional Authority: Public Schools as Mediating Structures," *Ohio State Law Journal 48* (1987): 663–731.
Hazelwood v. Kuhlmeier 484 U.S. 260 (1988)
International Society for Krishna Consciousness v. Lee, 505 U.S. 672 (1992)
Iowa Student Free Expression Law, *Iowa Code Sec. 280.22* (1989)
J.C. ex rel. R.C. v. Beverly Hills Unified School, 711 F. Supp. 2d 1094 (C.D. Cal. 2010)
Kansas Student Publications Act, *Kan. Stat. Ann. Sections 72.1504-72.1506* (1992)
Kincaid v. Gibson, 236 F. 3d 342 (6th Cir. 2001)
Massachusetts Student Free Expression Law, *Mass. Gen. Laws Ann. ch. 71, Section 82* (1988).

Miles v. Denver Public Schools, 944 F.2d 773 (10th Cir. 1991)
Oregon Student Free Expression Law (Public Secondary Schools), *Ore. Rev. Stat. sec. 336.477* (2007)
Oregon Student Free Expression Law (Public College and Universities), *Ore. Rev. Stat. sec. 351.649* (2007)
Pennsylvania Administrative Code: Student Rights and Responsibilities, *22 Pa. Code Section 12.9* (2005)
Spence v. Washington 418 U.S. 405 (1974)
Student journalists-Freedom of expression, *N.D. Cent. Code §15-10* (2015)
Texas v. Johnson 491 U.S. 397 (1989)
Tinker v. Des Moines Independent Community School District 393 U.S. 503 (1969)
Washington Administrative Code: Student Rights, *WAC 392-40-215* (1977).

CHAPTER 3

The Problems with Policies: The Ongoing Struggle between "Legal" and "Readable"

Abstract Schools create policies that inform students of prohibited behaviors so that should policies be broken, their students' due process rights will not be violated. While board and district policies are often widely available both offline and online, a majority of students are informed about their schools' policies through student handbooks. Translating policies crafted for adults to a language that connects with adolescents becomes a challenge worth pursuing. Salkin and Shenkel here begin to address the tension between legality and readability by reviewing the research on readability issues in a variety of policy environments ranging from online privacy to health and education.

Keywords Readability · Grade level · Policy language · Privacy policy

States, by virtue of the Tenth Amendment, are responsible for K-12 education.[1] Most states have invested a state educational agency with narrow legislative and executive authority to oversee educational operations.[2] Democratically elected school boards ensure local oversight of school districts and are given the responsibility to create local policies that ensure compliance with laws and policies created by the state agency.[3]

Such policies fill a constitutional role as well. The Due Process clause of the Fourteenth Amendment[4] assures citizens that they will not be deprived of life, liberty, or property without due process of the law. In 1975, the Supreme Court in *Goss v. Lopez*[5] noted that, by virtue of Ohio

© The Author(s) 2017

E. Salkin, L. Shenkel, *Student Speech Policy Readability in Public Schools*, DOI 10.1007/978-3-319-44132-0_3

state statutes mandating both the provision of a free education and compelled attendance (at public schools or private equivalents), the state had created a legitimate property and liberty right in access to such education.[6] As such, the Court determined that should a school decide to deprive a student of access to education in response to a prohibited activity, the school must first tell the student, "what he is accused of doing and what the basis of the accusation is."[7] It's reasonable to infer that an accusation must be tied to an existing policy, rule, or conduct code item—thus, schools create policies that inform students of prohibited behaviors so that should such policies be broken, their due process rights will not be violated.

What schools can take away from this dual responsibility to oversee education and protect due process is that there is strong legal support for schools creating policies and procedures that address student conduct. There is less guidance, however, on how to create or present such a policy. Many states mandate that districts distribute a student policy handbook or code of conduct annually to all students and parents (see Appendix 1), but do not offer guidance on the writing or presentation of the handbooks or codes themselves. In addition, there is no mandate to ensure that student handbooks or codes of conduct are written to be clear and grade-appropriate to their audiences.

A small but growing body of research literature on policy language in the modern era has explored the readability of policy statements that convey rights or responsibilities, to determine if the text of these important documents is crafted in such a way that it is understandable by the widest audience possible. A 2009 study of patient bill of rights documents created to satisfy Health Insurance Portability and Accountability Act (HIPAA)[8] requirements found that the documents had an average readability of 14th grade,[9] despite the fact that the average U.S. adult reads at an 8th-grade reading level.[10] HIPAA notification documents are mandated by law to ensure that people are informed of their right to privacy and to empower patients to make informed decisions about sharing medical information. The disparity between the readability of the written text and the capability of the average U.S. reader creates a very real concern—as the authors of the readability study note, "Efforts to cultivate communication skills and inculcate the importance of patient education in trainees are hampered by the mixed message presented by patients' rights documents that patients cannot read."[11]

In 2013, the same authors looked at consent forms used in medical schools to inform patients of their rights to opt in or out of medical research, and found a similar disconnect between the language of the consent form and the abilities of its audience.[12] Hospitals and clinics associated with medical schools provide a wide range of medical services and can be a lifesaving resource for patients who lack healthcare resources.[13] The lack of other options can put people who use medical school patient resources at risk of having their rights compromised. If patients believe they need to comply with all requests or they will not receive necessary care, and then they receive research participation consent forms written at a markedly higher readability level than the average U.S. adult reader has, it's difficult to ensure rights are protected. Educational institutions may be at risk as well, as it's plausible that such high readability levels may even contradict Institutional Review Board expectations that participants are able to understand the activities to which they are consenting.

Health information policies are not the only area of concern. Website privacy policies, which for some websites are mandated by the Federal Trade Commission, have also been studied for the match between readability and readership. A 2006 assessment of online privacy notice readability determined slightly more than half of the 312 website privacy policies evaluated were written at a level above high school reading level, despite the fact that 47.9 % of the U.S. adult population at the time did not have a college education.[14] The study tracked changes in the readability of these 312 privacy notices over a 2-year period, to see if user feedback led to revisions that improved readability, and found that 54 % of the policies became even more complex and difficult to read, while only 15 % saw a grade-level decline.[15]

An additional web privacy policy study in 2008 focused on the privacy policies of the 50 highest-traffic websites in the United States, and found an average readability grade level of 14.[16] A breakdown by industry found that insurance companies were the most readable (though still at a 13th-grade level) and pharmaceuticals the least readable (14.8).[17]

Within the educational environment, research has explored the readability of policies related to special education, with similar outcomes to those of health care and the web. For example, the Individuals with Disabilities in Education Act (IDEA)[18] requires schools to annually notify parents of the right to access educational support services for children who qualify. Because this is a federal mandate, it falls under a 1998 presidential executive order that requires government documents to be written in "plain language," which uses "common, everyday words, except for technical terms; 'you' and other pronouns; the active voice and short sentences."[19] A 2006 study sought to determine if IDEA documents actually met the readability expectations by examining language used to describe notice, mediation, and record-keeping in 50 different parents' rights documents. Researchers suggested that a 7th- to 8th-grade level was ideal, given statistics from the National Work Group of Literacy and Health that suggested half of American adults read at or below the 8th-grade level.[20] Instead, the study revealed more than 90 % of the documents reviewed read at higher than a 9th-grade reading level, potentially depriving parents and students in need of support services from the help that IDEA was designed to give them.[21] Further, a 2012 study looking at the same category of documents determined 40 % of the parent handouts required a graduate-school or professional-school level of reading skills to fully comprehend.[22] This project also noted that IDEA law encouraged children aged 16 or older to be a part of their educational planning, and subsequently the high-readability scores for existing documents also impacted those students' ability to understand their rights and responsibilities.

If policy readability is consistently a valid concern for adult audiences, it's reasonable to believe readability would be a similar, if not greater, concern for minors. If written texts that are created *by* adults, *for* adults, are consistently crafted at a readability level that surpasses roughly half of the U.S. adult population, would policies written by adults, but for youth, fare better? It's possible that the explicitly younger group—a grade-based group to boot—could force policy writers to think more specifically about their intended audience and intentionally engage in a language that fits the readers' abilities. However, policies create contractual obligations on the part of the school and the student, and need to be carefully created to accurately reflect the law. As stated already, public school student speech law is complex, and the application of First Amendment freedoms follows a winding path through key Supreme Court precedents and their lower court applications. Such complexity may drive up the readability on student speech policies.

NOTES

1. "The powers not delegated to the United States by the Constitution, nor prohibited by it to the States, are reserved to the States respectively, or to the people."
2. Kern Alexander & M. David Alexander, *American Public School Law* (6th ed.) (Belmont, CA: Thomson West, 2005), 108.
3. *Id* at 104.
4. U.S. CONST. amend. XIV.
5. 419 U.S. 565 (1975).

6. *Id.* at 573.
7. *Id.* at 582.
8. Pub.L. 104–191 (1996).
9. Michael K. Paasche-Orlow, Dan M. Jacob, Mark Hochhauser, & Ruth M. Parker, "National Survey of Patients' Bill of Rights Statutes," *Journal of General Internal Medicine* 24, no. 4 (2009): 491.
10. *Id* at 489.
11. *Id.* at 492.
12. Michael K. Paasche-Orlow, Frederick L. Brancati, Holly A. Taylor, Sumati Jain, Anjali Pandit, & Michael S. Wolf, "Readability of Consent Form Templates: A Second Look," *IRB: Ethics and Human Research* 35, no. 4 (2013): 12.
13. Joel Wesissman, Ernest Moy, Eric G. Campbell, Manjusha Gokhale, Recai Yucel, Nancyanne Causino and David Blumenthal, "Limited to the Safety Net: Teaching Hospital Faculty Report on their Patients' Access to Care," *Health Affairs* 22, no. 6 (2003): 156.
14. George R. Milne, Mary J. Culnan, & Henry Greene, "A Longitudinal Assessment of Online Privacy Notice Readability," *Journal of Public Policy and Marketing* 25, no. 2 (2006): 243.
15. *Id.*
16. Robert W. Proctor, M. Athar Ali, and Kim-Phuong L. Vu, "Examining Usability of Web Privacy Policies," *International Journal of Human–Computer Interaction* 24, no. 3 (2008): 319. Note that the study itself only included 47 policies, as three were unavailable.
17. *Id.* at 321.
18. Public L. No. 108–446 (2004).
19. Julie L. Fitzgerald & Marley W. Watkins, "Parents' Rights in Special Education: The Readability of Procedural Safeguards," *Exceptional Child* 72, no. 4 (2006): 499.
20. *Id.* at 506.
21. *Id.*
22. Carmen Gomez Mandic, Rima Rudd, Thomas Hehir, and Dolores Acevedo-Garcia. "Readability of Special Education Procedural Safeguards," *Journal of Special Education* 45, no. 4 (2012): 195.

References

Alexander, K., & Alexander, M. D., *American Public School Law* (6th ed.). Belmont, CA: Thomson West, (2005).

Fitzgerald, J. L., & Watkins, M. W., "Parents' Rights in Special Education: The Readability of Procedural Safeguards," *Exceptional Child 72*, no. 4 (2006): 497–510.

Goss v. Lopez 419 U.S. 565 (1975).

Health Insurance Portability and Accountability Act, Pub. L. 104–191 (1996).

Individuals with Disabilities in Education Act (IDEA), Pub. L. No. 108–446 (2004).

U.S. Constitution, Amendment XIV.

Mandic, C. G., Rudd, R., Hehir, T., & Acevedo-Garcia, D., "Readability of Special Education Procedural Safeguards," *Journal of Special Education 45*, no. 4 (2012): 195–203.

Milne, G. R., Culnan, M. J., & Greene, H., "A Longitudinal Assessment of Online Privacy Notice Readability," *Journal of Public Policy and Marketing 25*, no. 2 (2006): 238–240.

Paasche-Orlow, M. K., Jacob, D. M., Hochhauser, M., & Parker, R. M., "National Survey of Patients' Bill of Rights Statutes," *Journal of General Internal Medicine 24*, no. 4 (2009): 489–494.

Paasche-Orlow, M. K., Brancati, F. L., Taylor, H. A., Jain, S., Pandit, A., & Wolf, M. S., "Readability of Consent Form Templates: A Second Look," *IRB: Ethics and Human Research 35*, no. 4 (2013): 12–19.

Proctor, R. M., Ali, M. A., & Vu, K. L., "Examining Usability of Web Privacy Policies," *International Journal of Human-Computer Interaction 24*, no. 3 (2008): 307–328.

Wesissman, J., Moy, E., Campbell, E. G., Gokhale, M., Yucel, R., Causino, N., & Blumenthal, D., "Limited to the Safety Net: Teaching Hospital Faculty Report on their Patients' Access to Care," *Health Affairs 22*, no. 6 (2003): 156–166.

CHAPTER 4

Approaching the Question

Abstract To understand how students interpret their student handbook policies, Salkin and Shenkel used both content analysis and focus groups. The content analysis focused on language taken from randomly selected student handbooks from across the country. Once located, the handbook/code was reviewed for any text that indicated policy related to student speech/expression and student media or press: language specifically addressing the existence of the students' rights, including dress code. These sections were copied into a readability calculator. After these quantitative data were gathered, Salkin and Shenkel went into high school classrooms, giving students the same handbook language for reading and discussion. Those interpretations were evaluated for recurring themes and concepts.

Keywords Content analysis · Focus groups · FOG · ARI · Flesch-Kincaid

How public school students understand their free speech rights and responsibilities in their academic environments relies on several elements: *if* that information is presented expressly to them, *how* that information is presented expressly to them, and how that information is interpreted and applied *by* them. This multifaceted question requires a multifaceted approach.

© The Author(s) 2017   25
E. Salkin, L. Shenkel, *Student Speech Policy Readability in Public Schools*, DOI 10.1007/978-3-319-44132-0_4

The "If" and "How"

This project began with an analysis of student handbooks or codes of conduct created for public high school students. While student speech conflicts occur at every grade level, the courts tend to favor restriction for younger students because of the presumption of immaturity of preteens and younger. As a result, documents created for high school students offer a more intriguing and meaningful exploration of how students engage with the constitutional right to free speech.

Researchers began by identifying states that had statutes or administrative ordinances requiring school districts to create and disseminate school policies to students and teachers on a regular basis. From that subset, 15 states were randomly selected for analysis (see Appendix 1).

A list of public high schools was located on each state's educational agency website, and from that list, three high schools were selected using an online random list generator. Researchers visited each selected school's website and searched for a student handbook or code of conduct—if multiple documents were found, preference was given to the document that appeared to be regularly distributed to students and/or parents. The clearest indication of distribution was often a verification form on the second or last page of the handbook that students were asked to return with a parent's signature confirming the handbook had been received and reviewed.

School board or district policies were not consulted for this project, as they are not explicitly written for the student reader. While district-wide policies apply to students, and many districts encourage students to be familiar with policy guidance, the primary audience for these policies is adults: parents, teachers, administrators, and community members. Student handbooks or codes of conduct, on the other hand, are created to convey school board policies and building-specific rules particularly to students. That more focused intent for the content suggests the highest likelihood of student-friendly language: if any policies are going to be written at a student's comprehension level, they will be in the handbook created expressly for student use.

Once located, the handbook/code was downloaded and reviewed for any entries or text that clearly indicated policy related to student speech/expression and student media or press. The goal was to find language specifically addressing the existence and nature of the students' rights and responsibilities. As such, language that addressed conduct with speech implications (such as bullying or harassment) and language that included a speech element but did not define it, such as "No profanity in the halls," was not included.

This project also chose to exclude language that discussed speech occurring solely online. This may seem like an odd decision, given the rising problem that online speech presents to K-12 environments. Researchers were concerned, however, that policies applying only to online speech, such as social media, texting, or e-mail, would skew results by introducing speech-related regulation that is overshadowed by nonexpressive rationale, such as invasion of privacy, safety, and intellectual property. In addition, student speech rights as conveyed by the First Amendment apply regardless of platform—there is no separate First Amendment for the Internet. An analysis and discussion of cyberspeech policies is included in Chap. 7 as part of a larger application of this project's findings, but in general, policies regarding student speech rights need to be more focused on the act of expression than the medium in which it occurs.

For a point of comparison, each student handbook was also reviewed for language relating to the student dress code, which was selected because it is a common element in student policies and could be counted on to be regularly found. Further, several courts in recent years have acknowledged that student dress decisions have an expressive element.[1]

Sections that touched on these areas were copied in their entirety and pasted into an online readability calculator[2] to determine the following readability measures:

- Coleman–Liau index: This formula produces a grade-level readability score based on the average number of letters and sentences in the sample. It was initially developed to help assess textbooks, and often gives a lower score than other major readability standards.
- Flesch–Kincaid Grade Level: This formula produces a grade level of readability based on the number of syllables per word and words per sentence in the sample. It is one of the better-known readability measures, based out of work done for the Navy in the 1940s to improve the accessibility of training manuals.
- Automated Readability Index (ARI): ARI also calculates a grade level for readability, based on characters per word and words per sentence. It often scores higher than Coleman–Liau but lower than Flesch.
- Gunning-Fog Index: The fog index was developed by Robert Gunning to address the "fog" that dominated many newspapers

and business documents. It creates a grade level of difficulty based on syllables per word and words per sentence.[3]

Of these four, the Flesch–Kincaid grade level is the most widely used and highly correlated with other established readability scales.[4] The other two measures allow for a degree of confirmation and exploration of any possible variations.

The selected text was also examined qualitatively for common themes, structural similarities, and discussions of the motivation behind the policies. Any clear textual references to Supreme Court precedent, state laws, administrative policies intended to protect student speech or school discipline, or constitutional rights of students or children were noted and analyzed in the aggregate.

Finally, for contrast, a smaller sample of policies from private high schools in the same 15 states was examined using the same methodological approach. Private schools, as nongovernment entities, are not bound by the same First Amendment concerns as public schools. They are, however, education environments with the same social and cultural pressures. Could student speech policies be driven more by environmental factors than legal ones?

The three questions the textual analysis attempts to address are:

1. When student policy handbooks and/or codes of conduct address speech rights and responsibilities, how readable is the language used to describe those rights and responsibilities?
2. What are the common themes used in those policy/code statements and how does those themes relate to legal guidance on student speech?
3. Are student speech policies primarily driven by the constitutional mandate created by the *Tinker* decision, or by the educational environment and culture of modern secondary education?

THE "BY"

The second phase of this project sought to address the question of interpretation and application *by* students. While policies may be written with the intent that students understand and apply them appropriately, intentions do not always translate into results. To explore this question, researchers conducted five focus groups with public high school students, leading discussions that allowed for both interpretation and application of existing student speech or expression handbook entries.[5]

Each of the one-hour focus groups began with a brief overview of the four U.S. Supreme Court precedents that guide student speech law in public schools. The intent behind this initial discussion was to show students that student speech rights are not a unique, unknown concept that has never been discussed, but rather one with a degree of existing legal guidance.

After the overview, students were presented with two examples of student speech entries from their handbooks. Neither example came from the school or school district of the focus group participants:

Policy 1

Students are entitled to express their personal opinions verbally, symbolically, and in writing in a manner consistent with the First Amendment, considering the special nature of the school setting. True threats of violence and language or ideas of such a nature that it is reasonably probable that the expression will cause violent or unlawful behavior are not expression protected by the First Amendment and are not acceptable in the school setting.

Other forms of student expression that are not expressions protected by the First Amendment and are not acceptable in the school setting are expressions that are: (1) profane, vulgar, or obscene; (2) that reference illegal drug use, or that (3) will materially and substantially interfere with the maintenance and operation of the schools, including, but not limited to, the preservation of the educational process. Student expression that constitutes harassment or discrimination based on race, religion, color, national origin or ancestry, sex, gender identity, sexual orientation, age, marital or veteran status, or disability will not be tolerated.[6]

Policy 2

Students are entitled to express their opinions verbally, symbolically, and in writing. Student expression may not contain language or ideas that one could reasonably assume will create hostility, violence, or unlawful behavior; be it libelous, slanderous, profane, vulgar, or obscene; or materially or substantially interfere with the educational process.[7]

Students were given time to read the policies silently, then turn to a partner and discuss what they considered to be the strengths and weaknesses of the text. Finally, the entire group was brought together to share perspectives on what participants believed the policy allowed and prohibited, and how clear the language was for purposes of application.

After interpretation, the groups were asked to apply the second of the two policies to a hypothetical scenario based on Briana Popour's "Nobody Knows I'm a Lesbian" T-shirt. Students were presented with an image of a T-shirt that read "Nobody Knows I'm a Virgin" and were told that the student wearer was suspended for "engaging in disruptive expression while on school grounds." The groups were asked to reflect on the second policy and discuss if they believed that

1. the policy had been applied correctly, and
2. if the student should have anticipated the suspension based on the wording of the policy.

With any remaining time, students were tasked with brainstorming solutions to the common themes that emerged from the overall conversation. All focus groups were audio recorded for the purposes of later analysis, but students were asked to refrain from using names when referencing each other during discussion.

The recordings were reviewed by researchers for recurring concepts and ideas. While five focus groups of high school students totaling roughly 75 individuals cannot be called a statistically representative group, there were many consistent ideas and concepts expressed across the five groups that allowed for thoughtful, practical analysis.

NOTES

1. *See, e.g. Scott v. Napa Valley Unified Sch. Dist.*, No. 26-37082 (Calif. Super. Ct. Napa Co. prelim. injunction granted Jul. 2, 2007), in which a California court rejected a school dress code because it restricted student opportunities for expression.
2. Readability calculators are not consistent—there are dozens available online, and the same text element submitted to each one may result in different scores. The readability calculator selected, http://www.online-utility.org/english/readability_test_and_improve.jsp, was chosen because it was recommended by both the Association for Library Service to Children (ALSC) Education Committee (see http://ala13.ala.org/files/ala13/UnderstandingLevelingHandout.pdf) and the Harvard School of Public Health (http://www.hsph.harvard.edu/healthliteracy/practice/innovative-actions/).

3. Employment & Career Development Division, "Readability for Job Orders," *Washington State Employment Security Department website* (2011).
4. Julie L. Fitzgerald & Marley W. Watkins, "Parents' Rights in Special Education: The Readability of Procedural Safeguards," *Exceptional Child* 72, no. 4 (2006): 501.
5. IRB (Institutional Review Board) approval was secured before the focus groups were held, and all students completed consent forms (if 18 or older) or assent forms plus parental consent forms (if younger than 18). Student participants were promised confidentiality for their participation, but no other incentives were offered.
6. Tacoma Public Schools (Wash.), "Student Rights, Responsibilities and Regulations" (2010).
7. Bellingham Public Schools (Wash.), "Family Handbook and Calendar" (2015).

REFERENCES

ALSC Education Committee, "Understanding Leveling Systems," *American Library Association website* (2013).

Bellingham Public Schools (Wash.), "Family Handbook and Calendar" (2015).

Employment & Career Development Division, "Readability for Job Orders," *Washington State Employment Security Department website* (2011).

Fitzgerald, J. L., & Watkins, M. W., "Parents' Rights in Special Education: The Readability of Procedural Safeguards," *Exceptional Child 72*, no. 4 (2006): 497–510.

Harvard School of Public Health, "Assessing and Developing Health Materials," *Harvard T.H. Chan School of Public Health website* (n.d., last visited May 15, 2016).

"Readability Calculator," Online-Utility.org (last visited May 15, 2016).

Scott v. Napa Valley Unified Sch. Dist., No. 26 37082 (Calif. Super. Ct. Napa Co. prelim. injunction granted Jul. 2, 2007)

Tacoma Public Schools (Wash.), "Student Rights, Responsibilities and Regulations" (2010).

CHAPTER 5

Readability by the Numbers

Abstract Salkin and Shenkel located student handbooks or codes of conduct for three randomly selected high schools from 15 states, resulting in an overall sample of 45. These handbooks were plugged into a readability calculator in order to reveal Fog index, Coleman–Liau index, Flesch–Kincaid, and Automated Readability Index. Key takeaways from the numerical analysis showed that text discussing student's rights to expression or media is infrequently included and often crafted at a grade level higher than high school. Qualitative analysis of the content showed that there is strong deference to Supreme Court precedents in the rationale behind student speech policies.

Keywords Student handbooks · Readability · Expression · Media · Dress code

The first phase of this project focused on readability, or "the quality of written language that makes it easy to read and understand,"[1] of sections in student handbooks that address student speech or expression. Student handbooks or codes of conduct were successfully located on the websites of three randomly selected high schools from 15 states, resulting in an overall sample of 45 (see Appendix 2).

Reviewing the handbooks revealed inconsistent inclusion of language on student expression, media, and dress. Of the 45 handbooks, 42 included a

© The Author(s) 2017
E. Salkin, L. Shenkel, *Student Speech Policy Readability in Public Schools*, DOI 10.1007/978-3-319-44132-0_5

section on dress expectations or regulations, but only 23 addressed rights and responsibilities related to student expression. Further, only 10 outlined policies related to student publications. Of the total sample, eight handbooks (18 %) included statements addressing all three topics.

Reviewing the Numerical Data

Expression (N = 23): The average length of a section dealing with student rights to expression in the public school environment was 5 sentences or 112 words, resulting in an average of 22.4 words per sentence.[2] Reviewing the readability formulas are shown in Table 5.1.

None of the four readability formulas used in this study resulted in an average score for "expression" language that corresponded with the grade levels traditionally associated with high school. Reviewing the individual scores for each handbook revealed only *one* handbook's "expression" language scored at an appropriate grade level of 12 or lower on all four measurability scales. One handbook scored at a grade-appropriate level in three of the four scales, and five handbooks managed a grade-appropriate score in two of the four scales.

Overall, the key takeaway is:

Handbook language discussing student expression is inconsistently included, but consistently written at a more difficult level than its intended audience.

Media (N = 10): 22 % of the analyzed handbooks included language that identified rights and regulations related to student publications or media. The average length of these sections was eight and a half sentences or 162.8 words, resulting in an average of 19 words per sentence. The readability formulas for "media" are shown in Table 5.2.

Table 5.1 Readability of the student expression handbook entries

	Mean	Median	St. Dev.	GL[1] 9–12	GL 13–17	GL 18 +
Fog index	17.8	17.9	3.6	2	9	12
Coleman–Liau	14.4	14.4	2	3	17	3
Flesch–Kincaid	15.2	15.2	3.6	6	13	4
ARI	16.1	14.6	4.5	5	14	4

[1]"Grade Level" of readability.

Examined individually, no handbook "media" language consistently scored at an appropriate grade level (12 or lower) in all four readability scales. Two handbooks scored appropriately in three of four scales and another two scored appropriately in two scales. Only one handbook, from a high school out of Massachusetts, had both "expression" and "media" sections that were written at a high school grade-level readability by at least one readability scale. In other words, only 2 % of the sample included text on student rights and responsibilities related to expression and media that were written in a language easily understood by high school students.

Overall, the key takeaway is:

> Handbook language discussing student media is rarely included, and even more rarely written at a level consistent with the grade level of its intended audience.

Dress code ($N = 42$): All but three of the analyzed handbooks had a section outlining rights and expectations for student dress during the school day or school events. These sections had more content than sections covering expression and media—dress code sections had an average of 426.9 words or 29.9 sentences, resulting in 14.2 words per sentence. The readability formulas for "dress" are shown in Table 5.3.

Analyzing dress code language revealed that as many as a third of the handbook sections dedicated to this topic were written at a readability level *lower* than the level traditionally associated with high school. Nineteen handbook sections on dress code were written at a grade-appropriate level of 12 *or lower* in all four readability scales, and an additional 12 more scored at grade-appropriate levels in three of the four scales. A clear key takeaway is:

> Handbook language discussing student dress is consistently included and heavier on content, but at the same time is regularly presented at a level consistent with the grade level of its intended audience.

Table 5.2 Readability of the student media handbook entries

	Mean	Median	St. Dev.	GL 9–12	GL 13–17	GL 18 +
Fog index	16.89	15.36	4.7	0	7	3
Coleman–Liau	14.9	15.29	1.7	1	9	0
Flesch–Kincaid	14.2	13.57	4.4	4	5	1
ARI	14.6	13.6	5.5	4	5	1

Table 5.3   Readability of the student dress handbook entries

	Mean	Median	St. Dev.	GL 0–8	GL 9–12	GL 13–17	GL 18 +
Fog index	11.5	11.5	2.5	2	25	14	1
Coleman–Liau	12.1	11.5	1.6	0	24	18	0
Flesch–Kincaid	9.99	9.6	2.3	14	22	6	0
ARI	10.3	10.2	2.9	13	21	8	0

Comparing the readability results between the more difficult expression and media sections and the more grade-appropriate dress sections show that the differences are both notable and statistically significant (Table 5.4).

Overall, readability formulas indicate that language describing student expression and media, when present, is written above the grade level of its intended audience. This may be due, in part, to the higher word-to-sentence ratio, which is a number many of the measures used in this study rely on to calculate readability. Dress code, on the contrary, enjoyed a statistically significant lower readability level, averaging far closer to the readability levels of the actual students they are intended to serve.

LANGUAGE THEMES

Numbers give us some idea of readability, but the language and ideas used are equally, if not more, important to this project's analysis. High school students are on the verge of adulthood, and are less likely to accept a "Because I said so" rationale for regulation. High school handbooks need to ground the guidance on student rights and responsibilities within a reasonable rationale to get full buy-in by the student body.

Table 5.4   Comparing readability of dress handbook entries to expression entries and media entries

	Dress compared to Expression		Dress compared to Media	
	t (63)	P (2-tailed)	t (50)	P (2-tailed)
Fog	8.2059	.0001*	6.4138	.0001*
Coleman–Liau	5.1864	.0001*	3.2419	.00212*
Flesch–Kincaid	7.2762	.0001*	4.2539	.00092*
ARI	6.2475	.0001*	3.479	.00105*

*significant at p <.01

One immediate finding that emerges from this analysis is that student handbooks are clearly derived from school district policies. There are clear and regular references to school district or board policies throughout many student handbooks. This finding is cause for both celebration and concern: on the one hand, it establishes a consistent connection between the rules that guide the district and the rules that guide student behavior within a specific school. On the other hand, the connection to policy grounded in legal and administrative mandate increases the likelihood that language will be overly complex or complicated in order to stay faithful to the original. Both of these possibilities were observed after reviewing the text.

Expression: Twenty-three handbooks included some kind of language describing rights and regulations as related to student speech. Eleven of these handbooks, from seven different states, included language that directly reflected the "substantially interfere with the work of the school or impinge upon the rights of other students"[3] element of *Tinker v. Des Moines*, such as:

> Students' verbal and written expression of opinion on school premises is encouraged so long as it does not substantially disrupt the operation of the school.[4]

> For purposes of student speech, it is regulated here only insofar as it substantially disrupts or interferes with the work of the school or the rights of other students, is lewd, vulgar or profane, or is school- sponsored, i.e., speech that a reasonable observer would view as the school's own speech.[5]

Other handbooks attempted to define categories of speech open to school regulation, much like the approach taken in *Fraser* and *Morse*. For example, one handbook noted that, "The use of profanity, sexual innuendo/terms, and/or indecent gestures," was prohibited in any setting of the school.[6] Categorization resulted in some vagueness, however, as "inappropriate" language was prohibited in one school, while "G-rated" language was encouraged in another. While common-sense definitions to these terms would likely identify a majority of what is allowed and prohibited, the lack of clarity and omission of legitimate and exact definitions leaves a fair amount of gray area.

Structurally, many of the handbook sections addressing student expression were presented as block paragraphs comprising compound sentences. As noted in Chap. 3, many readability scores are based on number of words per sentence. A block paragraph structure lends itself to longer sentences, and subsequently contributed to the higher readability scores in the expression sections.

Media: Ten handbooks included language about student publication/media rights and regulations. Half of these handbook sections incorporated language reflective of *Tinker*, regulating publications or media that caused or were forecasted to cause a substantial disruption to the academic environment. For example:

> Written or printed material shall not be disseminated in such a way as to interfere with or interrupt the normal conduct of classes or the movement to and from classes.[7]

Only two handbooks—one from Arkansas and the other from Massachusetts—used language that connected with the *Hazelwood* precedent regarding student media. For example:

> Schools may limit the personal expression of students when school officials can show it is reasonably related to legitimate pedagogical concerns.[8]

It's worth noting that both Arkansas and Massachusetts have student publication protection statutes; in fact, 8 of the 10 handbooks that included student media language are from states with student press protection laws. Further, a separate handbook from Arkansas identified "forum" as a key determinant of regulation of student media, which suggests a connection to the reasoning of *Hazelwood*, though not incorporating a description of the reasonable-basis standard.

Two other recurring concepts from the student handbook sections on student publications were categories of speech subject to restriction and the possibility of prior review. Four handbooks specifically cited libel, obscenity, invasion of privacy, and poor journalistic quality as legitimate reasons for regulation of student publications or media—reasons reminiscent of *Hazelwood*, which noted that a school was allowed to disassociate itself from student speech that bears the school's imprimatur and is "ungrammatical, poorly written, inadequately researched, biased or prejudiced, vulgar or profane, or unsuitable for immature audiences."[9]

Half of the handbooks addressed the role of the publication adviser or administration in editorial decisions. Two handbooks assigned the role of "guide" to the adviser, while three explicitly noted that advisers and administrators have the ability to engage in prior review before a publication is printed or distributed on school grounds.

Structurally, the media sections looked much like the expression sections: block paragraphs with long sentences. Again, this likely contributed to their higher readability scores.

Dress. All but three of the handbooks evaluated included language on appropriate dress for the academic environment. The dress code sections were a far better match to the high school grade-level readability than the expression or media sections were, and structure likely contributed strongly to that difference. A majority of the dress code sections began with a statement of purpose detailing the reason for the dress code, then outlined dress expectations in a bulleted or numbered list of short phrases or sentences. Multiple examples were given of prohibited items or styles of dress, also in short sentences and straightforward language.

Two strong themes emerged behind the rationale for a dress code. One was health and safety: slightly more than half of the handbooks regulated clothing to minimize accidents or opportunities for injury. Even more prevalent, however, was the declaration that dress could be regulated to prevent a disruption to the orderly functioning of the school—the *Tinker* standard. Thirty-three of the 42 handbooks included some variation of this language to support the need for a dress code. This inclusion might suggest that schools see dress as a form of expression, as the courts have, and six handbooks explicitly note that student choices in dress and appearance are forms of expression (one example: "Students have a right to express themselves through dress and personal appearance"[10]).

Beyond these two recurring themes, a few additional ideas are seen in several handbooks to justify the regulation of student dress and appearance, including alignment with community standards, the desire to project a positive self-image or image of the school, a concern for explicit messages on clothing (such as language on T-shirts) and the opportunity to teach respect for authority.

CONTRASTING AGAINST PRIVATE SCHOOLS

Public schools are required to comply with the dictates of the First Amendment—private schools, as nongovernment actors, are not. To explore if the constitutional mandate is a primary driver of student handbook language, a selection of student handbooks from private high schools in the same 15 states was evaluated for expression, media, and dress to get a comparative data set.

Thirty-five student handbooks from private high schools were located online and evaluated using the same approach as the public school handbooks. Eight of the schools were secular, seven were Catholic, and the rest identified broadly as Christian. Eleven handbooks included language on student expression, two included language on student media, and all 35 addressed student dress.

The differences in readability scores between private and public student handbooks were not statistically significant in sections related to expression or media, but were significant for dress codes, as by every readability measure the private dress codes resulted in *lower*-grade-level readability than the public (Table 5.5).

The qualitative exploration of private student handbook language revealed some similarities between public and private when looking at expression and media. Three of 10 private student handbooks addressing student expression used the "disruption/interference" language of *Tinker* to describe possible regulation of student speech. Another five used the categorical approach seen in several public handbooks to describe types of speech prohibited in the academic environment. Because many of the private schools were religiously affiliated, the motivation behind their regulations was often expressed as a faith-based responsibility to God or the Bible. The two handbooks that discussed student publications or media both addressed the question of prior review, granting administrators and advisers the express ability to demand changes or prohibit printing/distribution.

The dress code sections were longer and more detailed than in public handbooks. Many of the private student handbooks broke dress code

Table 5.5 Comparing readability of public and private school dress handbook entries

	Mean (private)	Mean (public)	t (75)	P (2-tailed)
Fog	9.740285714	11.55333333	3.8248	0.000269*
Coleman-Liau	10.54	12.06261905	4.4014	0.000035*
Flesch–Kincaid	8.195428571	9.999047619	4.0539	0.000122*
ARI	8.22	10.29928571	3.7011	0.000407*

*significant at p <.01

down by gender, listing allowable or prohibited clothing by item (shirts, pants, etc.) or by style (tight, baggy, revealing, etc.). Separate sections for field trips, chapel days, formal events, and performances were also included in several handbooks.

The motivations behind dress regulations deviated from the public handbooks. Where the public schools focused on a *Tinker*-based disruption of education element as well as health and safety, the 35 private school handbooks primarily rationalized a dress code by referencing a duty to God (11) or a desire for modesty in dress (9). While a concern for the academic environment was expressed in several handbooks, the focus was less on "disruption/interference" and more on the particular ideals of a productive, appropriate learning community.

Some handbooks suggested that a dress code also benefited the academic environment by:

- Reflecting "gender distinctiveness;"
- Indicating "self-respect and courtesy for others;"
- Showing "respect for authority;"
- Presenting "a school-business atmosphere; school is the 'job' of our students;"
- Providing "an equal standing among students from diverse economic backgrounds;" or
- Discouraging "the use of clothing as a significant means of establishing self-identity or gaining attention or social status."

Not surprisingly, private school student handbooks appear to be far less driven by First Amendment or free speech concerns, even when discussing issues related to free speech, expression, or press. Instead, regulations appear to be driven by the needs of the specific school and its educational mission.

Takeaways

While no single study will definitively solve student handbook readability questions, the results of this exploration do suggest some intriguing directions. Centering the analysis on student handbooks allowed a focus on documents specifically created for students. School districts certainly have written policies to guide all of the schools, teachers, and students under their jurisdiction on issues of expression, publication, and dress rights of students, but these statements of policy were not explicitly written for a student audience. Student handbooks are written for the student audience, as evidenced by the requirement that students sign and return an affidavit that they read and understand handbook policies at the start of every school year.[11]

Revisiting the three questions this phase of the project sought to answer:

1. When student policy handbooks and/or codes of conduct address speech rights and responsibilities, how readable is the language used to describe those rights and responsibilities?
2. What are the common themes used in those policy/code statements and how does those themes relate to legal guidance on student speech?
3. Are student speech policies primarily driven by the constitutional mandate created by the *Tinker* decision, or by the educational environment and culture of modern secondary education?

How readable is the language? Four readability formulas developed to attach grade levels to text indicated that the language used by most public school student handbooks to describe student expression and student media rights is written at a level that is beyond the average high school student's ability to quickly read and understand. This isn't to say that a student could not understand the text after a close rereading and thoughtful reflection upon a given passage. However, as with any written element, readers generally will not invest the time into fully understanding complex texts unless they already have a strong motivation to do so. If handbooks are to proactively inform students of their speech and publication rights prior to issues becoming problems, readability must be grade-appropriate in order to capture the largest possible audience.

Writing student expression and media policies at a reading level more suited for university undergraduates poses real problems for the high school academic environment. While many students likely understand that speech qualifying as "bullying" or "harassment" carries penalties, a lack of clear, comprehensible guidance on expression that conveys ideas (as opposed to expression that equals conduct[12]) means students are at a loss as to their rights to freely speak within the academic environments that claim much of their days. As a result, there is either a hesitancy to engage in expression—self-censorship for fear of an unclear regulation—or disillusionment when students are penalized for expression that they believed had a level of protection. The result of both is a misunderstanding of fundamental free speech tenets that may easily carry over into their adult lives, and a disruption of their education, which should be their primary focus.

Comparing the expression/media language to dress code language shows that schools are more than capable of writing handbook language at a grade-appropriate level. While elements of *Tinker* and other speech precedents are present in the language used for handbook sections on expression or media, they are not so overwhelming of each section that we can attribute the overwriting to "legalese" sneaking its way into student handbooks. The dress code sections, which also frequently reference *Tinker*, show that policy can be written at (or even below) high school reading levels.

What are the common themes? All three categories of language examined for this study—expression, media, and dress—saw significant use of the *Tinker* standard to formulate language, rationalize policy, and define prohibitions on speech, press, or dress. The repeated emphasis on this key legal authority suggests the public school student handbooks are primarily motivated by the law when it comes to clarify the potentially expressive rights of students. While some educational environment issues came into play regarding dress codes (for example, health and safety), and sociological factors were also evident (community norms, representation of the school), the strongest influence was clearly common law interpretation of public school student rights to expression.

Many handbooks alluded to school board or district policies, supporting the idea that common-law student media precedents are a significant motivator for handbook language, as most of these board/district policies are written to ensure compliance with federal and state law.

Structurally, the dress code sections in the public school student handbooks appeared to be written for greater comprehension than the expression/media sections. Many of these sections included a statement of purpose and some form of bulleted or numbered list that gave clear guidance, backed with examples, of allowed or prohibited items and styles. A high school student reading these sections would come away with a clear reason for the policy and opportunities to compare his or her clothing/appearance decisions to examples of allowable dress. Most dress codes also included language allowing administration the flexibility to act in unique circumstances and the ability to make individual determinations of appropriateness as they see fit, thus protecting the ability to respond in the moment when the dress code does not adequately address a given situation.

The dress code shows that handbook language covering an expressive element can be written with clarity and purpose to give students a sense of what is allowed and prohibited at a grade level of readability that fits their general comprehension. Unfortunately, such an approach does not filter into sections on expression or press (when they are present at all), depriving students of the assurance of their ability to engage with ideas in their academic environments.

What appears to drive public school student speech policies? This phase of the project also looked at private school student handbooks as a point of comparison: if similar themes appeared in private school handbooks, then the driving force behind decisions related to student expression, media, and dress might be extralegal. The qualitative analysis of relevant handbook selections at private high schools, however, revealed a far more internal motivation behind regulations on student expression, media, or dress. Such policies were driven more by the school's independent mission, its religious mission, or its perceived role within its communities. While some *Tinker*-based language popped up in a few handbooks, it was clearly the minority compared to language referencing a student's duty to his or her educational environment, fellow students, or God. The motivation for public schools, then, appears to be closely aligned to constitutional responsibilities.

Notes

1. *Readability*. Webster's-Dictionary.org (n.d.).
2. However, the median word count was 75, indicating an outlier effect.
3. *Tinker* 393 U.S. at 509.
4. Everett Public Schools (Wash.), "Student Responsibilities & Rights Policies" (2014).
5. Twin Valley School District (Pa.), "TVHS Student Handbook" (2014).
6. Palmyra-Eagle Area School District (Wis.), "Palmyra-Eagle High School Student Handbook" (2011).
7. Pomeroy Junior-Senior High School (Wash.), "Pirate Log Student/Parent Handbook" (2014).
8. West Bridgewater Public Schools (Mass.), "Student Handbook" (2014).
9. *Hazelwood* 484 U.S. at 271.

10. Del Norte School District C-7 (Colo.), "High/Middle School Student Handbook" (2014).
11. If they actually do so—much like the question of how often people read terms and use policy before clicking "I agree" online—is a question for another day.
12. *Spence v. Washington* (418 U.S. 405, 1974) describes the difference between "expression" and "conduct" well: we have expression that is open to First Amendment protection if "an intent to convey a particularized message was present, and in the surrounding circumstances the likelihood was great that the message would be understood by those who viewed it." *Spence* at 410–11.

References

Del Norte School District C-7 (Colo.), "High/Middle School Student Handbook" (2014).
Everett Public Schools (Wash.), "Student Responsibilities & Rights Policies" (2014).
Hazelwood v. Kuhlmeier, 484 U.S. 260 (1988)
Palmyra-Eagle Area School District (Wis.), "Palmyra-Eagle High School Student Handbook" (2011).
Pomeroy Junior-Senior High School (Wash.), "Pirate Log Student/Parent Handbook" (2014).
Readability. Webster's-Dictionary.org (n.d.).
Spence v. Washington, 418 U.S. 405 (1974).
Tinker v. Des Moines Independent Community School District, 393 U.S. 503 (1969).
Twin Valley School District (Pa.), "TVHS Student Handbook" (2014).
West Bridgewater Public Schools (Mass.), "Student Handbook" (2014).

CHAPTER 6

Students Weigh in: Application and Interpretation by the Target Audience

Abstract Salkin and Shenkel spent time in high school classrooms, giving students the opportunity to review, apply, and improve samples of language used by student handbooks to describe student speech right and responsibilities, as well as reflect on what they mean for them, as students. Their responses gave way to recurring themes: the idea that intention matters in the context of expression and that terms and concepts within handbook language should be as clear as possible in order to increase the chances of appropriate and harmless expression.

Keywords Cultural norms · Interpretation · Focus groups · Definitions · Intent

Readability and content analysis only get us so far, and they present a similar problem to the core of this study: adults interpreting the comprehensiveness of policy rather than the students engaging in interpretation and meaning making. Tweaking words and sentences could reduce Fog indexes to appropriate grade levels, but that alone does not ensure that policies are relatable to the students they were created to serve.

The next step of this exploration takes place in the classroom. Several groups of high school students had the opportunity to review, apply, and improve samples of student speech policies as presented in student handbooks, and reflect upon what those policies meant to them. Their

© The Author(s) 2017

E. Salkin, L. Shenkel, *Student Speech Policy Readability in Public Schools*, DOI 10.1007/978-3-319-44132-0_6

responses confirmed the findings of a broad spectrum of research: schools are unique environments with lifeworlds all their own. Speech rights, like any element within this complex culture, must respond to the social pressures exerted by the multiple layers that exist between and among students, teachers, administrators, and staff.

A RECURRING THEME: INTENT MATTERS

In Murray Milner Jr.'s *Freaks, Geeks and Cool Kids*, the author stressed the role of conformation to the social norm in adolescent society. His research indicated that these norms emerged from careful deliberation within teen culture, and were often rooted specifically within the high school experience. He urged caution about the adult (teacher/administrator/staff) role within this norm creation. We are left with this question: Do adult efforts to shape social norms within adolescent worlds, like high schools, unfairly impact teens' personal and social autonomy?[1] In other words, should adults give teens space to develop the rules and norms that regulate their relationships with each other?

The responses by students in the focus groups show that Milner's question of student autonomy and high school culture is relevant to this study. Participants discussed how they felt they had both the right and responsibility to set the social norms that guided their student culture, and wanted speech regulations to reflect their social expectations, not just administrator perspectives. This was most clearly seen in a recurring demand to understand intent. It wasn't enough for a student to know what was said, they wanted to know and understand the intent *of the student speaker* behind the words before they were willing to pass judgment—and they wanted policies to do the same.

> I think if it's done intentionally to either hurt or frustrate or like anything intentionally against someone or like a group of people then definitely they need to be talked to but if the person doesn't think about the other person and it's not like intended to hurt them in any way then I think they should get a warning and be like "Hey you should think about other people."

Students recognized the likelihood of misinterpretation when they speak with each other, and wanted the policies that govern their expression to allow for room to reconcile intended messages with received messages. Far more intriguing, however, was the student expectation behind intent.

Speech that caused mere discomfort, challenged deeply held opinions, or pushed boundaries was all fine. Speech that was thoughtless or directly aimed at an individual with the intent to cause harm was not:

> It all boils down to don't say something stupid. That's just the thing that's understood by students. This is just outlining what is stupid and what isn't.

> I think if it's done intentionally to hurt or frustrate someone, then it definitely should not be ok. But if it wasn't done against another person, not to hurt them, then I think they should get a warning and think about what the impact of their words is.

> You have the general idea of what you can say because you know the other students. But that doesn't come from the handbook.

It appears that Mom's classic, "If you can't say anything nice, don't say anything at all," still holds weight with students, but such a finding is not wholly unexpected. Past research with preadolescents and adolescents suggests that middle and high school students are drawn to acts of kindness and adapt social norms to reward such acts. For example, a study involving 9- to 11-year-olds found that students who performed three acts of kindness per week over the course of four weeks not only enjoyed an increased sense of well-being and self-esteem, but also experienced an increase in peer acceptance.[2] The authors noted that prosocial behavior "has a strong positive association with later peer acceptance, and this relationship is likely bidirectional, as children who feel accepted are more likely to do things for others, and, in turn, children who do things for others might gain the acceptance of their peers."[3]

Whether it was conscious or not, students in these focus groups consistently wanted their student speech policy to accurately reflect a social norm of kindness, with intent as a key factor in assessing if speech has crossed the line from merely annoying to something actionable. If there is intent to be cruel and break the prosocial norm, then such speech stands in the way of student learning and should be subject to discipline.

Many students, by high school, have learned to navigate the differences between authority figures, such as teachers and administrators, and their peers. They understand that lateral communication among equals will be held to different standards and criteria than vertical communication between students and teachers. Yet, students reliably noted that existing student speech policies did not clarify if—or how—that kind of context was accounted for when analyzing the potential impact of student speech.

While they acknowledged that there were types of expression one could share with a friend that would not be appropriate to share with a teacher, they also recognized that speech could have a real impact on their education. As a result, they wanted to see that a student speech policy would account for the different expectations and potential impact of lateral versus vertical speech. Context mattered in the form of intent and impact, and student participants wanted to see that context and intentionality addressed in their policies:

> Let's say someone is putting notes in a locker. If it's something educational, like "here's this fun little fact that can improve your day," then hey, that's cool. Even if you don't like it, it's no big deal. Forcing an idea on somebody— if that note was trying to force a specific opinion of idea, like if that note was a religious-based, and somebody decided that everybody needs to listen to this, then that's something that shouldn't be allowed, because then you're infringing on somebody else's freedom.

> If everyone around us is learning and we're ok with it, but she [a teacher] isn't ok with it, how does it hurt us? We're still going to learn no matter what. If it just affects the teacher, not the students, then it shouldn't matter.

STUDENTS SAY: LANGUAGE RAISES CONCERNS

As students dove into the two sample speech policies provided (see Appendix 3) and attempted to apply them to the scenario presented, a recurring concern about definitions came into play. Once again, a strong concern about social norms was raised, as students wanted to know not only what the definitions of key words were, but also who was responsible for creating and maintaining the definitions.

For example, both policies used the phrase, "materially or substantially interfere with the educational process," a clear reference to the *Tinker* precedent. Students were unclear what might qualify as such an act of interference and began offering their own definitions of a distraction:

> If it actually makes somebody, or causes distraction—was there actually a rally in the hallways, or was it just one teacher that was upset? You have to be taking away from someone. We're talking about our education going to be affected.

From there, the students began to question the required breadth of an act of interference. Some suggested that interference with just one person's education was enough to warrant school action, while others suggested that a more widespread impact was necessary for speech to be actionable:

> It should be more large-scale—there could be one student who doesn't like it, and that's student-centered, so the school would be like "go home." Disruption of the academic process should mean that it means the whole class can't learn, not just one person.

> We all have the right to learn, we all have a right to an education. So if it's something that's infringing on the right to an education, then that's when it's wrong, and that's when it should be considered punishable.

Another problematic phrase to students in these focus groups was "language or ideas that one could **reasonably assume**." Students questioned the "reasonable" standard because it failed to provide context for either speaker or audience. Whose "reasonable assumption" is more important—the person speaking or the audience exposed to hostility, violence, or unlawful behavior? Further, who gets to make the determination that the assumption is reasonable—students, who are familiar with the context of peer-to-peer communication, or teachers? As participants noted:

> I think they need to define who is "assuming," what is "assuming"— because they just say "could reasonably assume," but they could change it to say "that the school administration could assume," or that a "student could reasonably assume."

> If they choose to keep "assume," they need to put from whose perspective it is. If it is just a third party, that they would reasonably assume that that comment is going to be offensive, they need to specify that.

One student noted that, with that kind of phrase, an administrator could argue that anything is actionable—the policy created too many realistic scenarios that would lead to the punishment of everyday speech. In law, such language would be problematic under what is known as "vagueness doctrine:" a rule that requires criminal laws to state explicitly and definitely what conduct is punishable so the average person can know what actions fall within its boundaries.[4] When dealing with student speech, vagueness becomes a special concern, as research indicates that students who are uncertain of their speech rights are more likely to remain silent rather than risk punishment.[5] As one student participant noted:

> I don't know what my rights are. When reading that, I don't know what I can and can't do, and when you don't know what your rights are, then punishments can be added in without correct jurisdiction—so I don't feel like they're being protected when I don't even know what they are in this case.

While students were willing to define the general intent behind student speech policies as "don't do anything mean," they reflected a consistent concern for the explicit crafting and application of such policies. Students were willing to concede a common-sense purpose behind policies, but were not willing to allow such breadth in the language used to define those policies. While they acknowledged that no one can craft a this'll-solve-every-conceivable-problem policy, they hoped to see specific language that would help them understand how policies would be applied and how conflicts in interpretation might be resolved:

> I think that it all just has to come down to being more specific, because there are times when, I don't know, maybe you check the student handbook because you think that your t-shirt is questionable, and you check the handbook and you think this is ok—to me, this isn't slanderous or anything, so you wear the shirt and you go to school—you need to be more explicit about what's going to affect others.

> I don't think there's a way to list out all the things you can and cannot do. There's always going to be things that offend people that for others it doesn't. You have to find a way to work around it.

Toward the end of each discussion, students kept coming back to the question of how student speech policies and restrictions fit into their overall education. The question has merit—many studies have suggested that students who feel empowered to share their opinions freely within their educational environment are more engaged with learning, as well as with their communities and civic responsibilities.[6] There is an educational benefit to student free speech, and while that line of research was not discussed during these focus groups, students had the sense that speech restriction needed purpose beyond concern for disruption:

> It's about how the institution is setting you up for the real world. This kind of approach doesn't help. How does this prepare you for the real world?

I don't understand what the issue is. Are they afraid that speech will interfere with education? If so, shouldn't they just teach people to be more tolerant?

There was also a perception of hypocriticism. Students acknowledged that some speech—primarily violent speech, false/slanderous speech, and obscenity—would be regulated without debate under the sample policies given. What they were not as sure about was speech that discussed sexual activity among their peers, drug use, religious differences, sexuality, or politics. All of these topics not only have the potential to create disruption, but are also topics of classes that students are required to take as part of the state-mandated curriculum:

> They treat us like we don't know what customs are and stuff. We know that, since we're tiny. Like they say don't use bad words, don't wear stuff that talks about drugs—they teach us that stuff in health and fitness when we're freshmen. So we can't say or wear things like that. It seems kind of hypocritical, that they teach us about it but we aren't supposed to talk about it.

The student participants brought an exciting and intriguing depth of social expectation and opportunity to their discussions of student speech policies. Their conversations showed the need to address the social norms of the students and their greater community when crafting handbook language that describes policy. If a policy is created and enforced with that intention, it will more likely support the norm that the community has already manifested and be more usable (and understandable) to the student audience it was created to inform.

Ultimately, all involved parties benefit from such an approach. Students have clarity and investment in the speech policies that govern their in-school expression and teachers have confidence in their ability to regulate a forum of student expression that enhances the learning environment. All parties get to enjoy the positive impact of free expression on the educational environment—or as a teacher in 1903 wrote:

> Expression in education means all that it does in life. It is work developed by community interests; it is a social function, and should serve the social organism. There must be a real demand felt by the child for what he produces…Expression is a necessity of growth. The tendency of all thought is to manifest itself in some kind of form. Its vitality depends largely upon its embodiment in expression…Free expression reacts to intensify, clarify, and vivify thought.[7]

NOTES

1. Milner Jr., M., *Freaks, Geeks and Cool Kids: American Teenagers, Schools and the Culture of Consumption* (New York: Routledge, 2004).
2. K. Layous, S.K. Nelson, E. Oberle, K.A. Schonert-Reichl and S. Lyubomirsky. "Kindness Counts: Prompting Prosocial Behavior in Preadolescents Boosts Peer Acceptance and Well-Being," *PLoS ONE 7*, no. 12: e51380. doi: 10.1371/journal.pone.0051380 (2012).
3. *Id.*
4. Legal Information Institute. "Vagueness doctrine," *Cornell University Law School website* (n.d., last visited May 15, 2016).
5. Matt Wynn. "Threat of censorship has 'chilling effect.'" *Quill* 90, no. 3 (2002): 40.
6. P.S. Bobkowski & P.R. Miller. "Civic implications of secondary school journalism: Associations with voting propensity and community volunteering," *Journalism and Mass Communication Quarterly*, published online before print doi: 10.1177/1077699016628821 (2016).
7. Martha Fleming. "Expression," *The Elementary School Teacher* 3, no. 8 (1903): 544.

REFERENCES

Bobkowski, P. S., & Miller, P. R., "Civic implications of secondary school journalism: Associations with voting propensity and community volunteering", *Journalism and Mass Communication Quarterly*, published online before print doi: 10.1177/1077699016628821 (2016).

Fleming, M., "Expression", *The Elementary School Teacher 3*, no. 8 (1903): 543–549.

Layous, K., Nelson, S. K., Oberle, E., Schonert-Reichl, K. A., & Lyubomirsky, S., "Kindness Counts: Prompting Prosocial Behavior in Preadolescents Boosts Peer Acceptance and Well-Being", *PLoS ONE 7*, no. 12: e51380. doi: 10.1371/journal.pone.0051380 (2012).

Legal Information Institute. "Vagueness doctrine", *Cornell University Law School website* (n.d., last visited May 15, 2016).

Milner Jr., M., *Freaks, Geeks and Cool Kids: American Teenagers, Schools and the Culture of Consumption*. New York: Routledge, (2004).

Wynn, M., "Threat of censorship has 'chilling effect,' ", *Quill 90*, no. 3 (2002): 40.

CHAPTER 7

Applying These Findings to Student Handbooks and Student Speech

Abstract In this chapter, Salkin and Shenkel concisely summarize their research findings while qualitatively evaluating student interpretations to student handbook policies. They link these findings to how a student handbook can ultimately be improved and lead to more rewarding classroom environments. Additionally, they address these findings in the realm of cyberspeech and social media, an area of expression that is rapidly becoming a significant challenge for public school administrators, teachers, and students alike. This chapter also addresses the critical "why" of student speech policy within student handbooks, discussing the legal, educational, and cultural benefits of clarity about speech rights.

Keywords Student handbooks · Readability · Cyberspeech · Social media · Policy

Briana Popour is not the first and will surely not be the last young adult to receive pushback for personal expression while in school, which is why this topic of clarity and connection between student speech policies and the students they are meant to serve is so important. Rather than focusing on enacting punishments in response to the damage that expression can inherently cause, this project suggests a far more proactive approach: taking the student speech policies that likely already exist within a school

© The Author(s) 2017   55
E. Salkin, L. Shenkel, *Student Speech Policy Readability in Public Schools*, DOI 10.1007/978-3-319-44132-0_7

district and using them to craft meaningful entries in the handbooks that already go out to the student body.

In the case of Popour and many others that left an impression on a classroom, there was a disconnect between what the student handbook intended to convey about speech and expression rights/responsibilities and what the student understood. The aim of this project was to dive into that disconnect and seek ways to bridge the gap. Through content analysis of existing handbooks and focus groups with high school students, this project sought to answer:

1. Do handbooks take up the topic of expression at all?
2. If they do, how "readable" is the presentation of student expression rights and responsibilities?
3. How do students interpret and apply handbook entries on student expression?

The first two questions were addressed by the first phase of the project: a content analysis of student handbooks from a randomly selected group of public high schools from across the country. This analysis revealed that student speech—either personal expression or student media—is not reliably addressed in student handbooks. Only half of the 45 handbooks reviewed included some kind of specific content on student speech rights or responsibilities, and far fewer included text describing student media rights.

A selection of four mainstream readability calculators revealed that those handbooks that did include language on student expression or media rights crafted those sections at a grade level that surpassed the levels of the students under their charge. Average grade levels of the readability of these sections ranged from 14 to 16, or a better fit to undergraduate college/university students than high school students. The structure of these sections likely contributed to their high grade-level readability measurements, as most were presented as block paragraphs of lengthy sentences.

The content analysis also reviewed dress codes for a point of comparison. One of the most significant takeaways from this comparison is that student handbook entries can be and are written at an appropriate grade level for their students. Dress code sections ranged in readability from a high nine to a low 12; an excellent fit to a high school audience. The structure of these policies likely contributed to their lower scores, as they were more often built as bulleted lists of short sentences with active language.

From content analysis, this project moved into an interpretation and application phase by meeting with high school students to explore how they interacted with student speech sections from handbooks. This was an opportunity to see what content analysis could not tell us—how the students in real time and real life felt they could use these handbook entries as they evaluate their own speech.

The students in these focus groups were eager and willing to share their reactions to the handbook policies they were given. Students felt strongly that policies as presented in their handbooks should give them clear direction about both the rights and responsibilities they had regarding free speech within their educational environments. A handful of common themes quickly emerged:

- Students quickly picked out vague terms or phrases and had difficulty coming to consensus about what they believed those terms or phrases meant.
- Context mattered. Students recognized that the educational experience is not homogeneous, and wanted to know how the policies as stated in the handbooks recognized that speech in different contexts (such as the classroom, hallway, or school bus) would be assessed relative to that context.
- Building off of the context question, students wished to know if and how their own input would come into the assessment of prohibited speech. They had no issue with a teacher deeming speech appropriate or inappropriate for a classroom conversation, but they noted that the speech that occurs between and among students in other parts of the academic environment might be shaped more by the social norms that the students themselves have created. As such, it would be more accepted by students than the teachers or administrators, and deserved different treatment from in-class speech.

The focus groups findings supported those of the content analysis in several ways. First, researcher observation saw that student participants needed to read and reread the policy to begin to grasp its meaning. The block-paragraph, long-sentence approach worked against readability. Students confirmed that vague terms, which were identified through content analysis as potentially problematic, were indeed issues that inhibited interpretation and application.

What the focus groups brought that no amount of content analysis could reveal is the importance of the cultural element when discussing student speech rights and responsibilities. School board and district policies are grounded in law to ensure that they comply with the U.S. Constitution, Supreme Court common law, and any applicable state statutes. When these policies are included in student handbooks, however, students want to see both the legal and the cultural elements addressed. This is equally important as word and syllable counts—students believe acknowledgment of the norms and culture of their community enhances the usability of a given policy, thereby improving its readability and ability to be applied.

The cultural element of readability hasn't been extensively studied in the academic environment, but it isn't an entirely new concept. Several researchers have explored how cultural norms impact readability of medical information, such as cancer prevention or treatment materials.[1] In this project, the idea of including cultural norm language in handbook language discussing student speech and expression offers fascinating insight on what students need to bridge the gap between where they are and where the adults in their academic lives believe them to be. Being guided by social norms is innate to individuals, adolescents in particular, and letting a school handbook language reflect that only improves the role this language was created to fill.

The Cyber-Elephant in the Room

Any guidance on student speech in public schools in the modern era must address the complication of cyberspeech. As discussed in Chap. 2, the Supreme Court has yet to give definitive legal guidance on the approach mandated by the First Amendment to public school student cyberspeech. The challenge is the off-campus genesis of most online speech, both in terms of both physical location and time of day. Can, or perhaps the better question is *should*, a school regulate the speech of students when those students are not physically present on school grounds or under the direct authority of school officials? How can the findings of this project help such regulation be accurately portrayed within a student handbook?

Many schools already attempt to express some sort of cyberspeech regulation within their student handbooks. Thirty-five of the 45 student handbooks analyzed for this project included a statement on cyberspeech, ranging from a brief 65-word mention to a more impressive 2500-word description of permissible online activity, which included 20 categories of prohibited online speech.[2]

Within these handbook entries on online activity and speech were several consistent categories of speech that were considered punishable: copyright infringement (15), cyberbullying (12), discrimination (8), harassment (17), illegal (8), libel/defamation (7), obscenity (23), profanity (7), and threats (11). Thirteen policies explicitly noted that students did not have a right to privacy when engaging in speech that used the school's or district's equipment or network, and another eight prohibited the use of either equipment or network to engage in political lobbying or commercial activities.

The structure of these entries more closely mimicked the dress codes than the student speech/publication entries explored in Chap. 5, in that they presented as bulleted or numbered lists with specific statements about allowed and disallowed activities. The readability analysis, however, still trended high, as can be seen in Table 7.1:

From a readability perspective, current cyberspeech student handbook language still suffers from the same issues as general student speech policies: overly complex sentences written to comply with district policies and state and federal laws, regardless of the specific student audience for which they are crafted.

Similar issues arise with a content review of these student handbook entries. Most are rooted in the categorical approach, identifying the types of speech that are generally considered to be prohibited and/or actionable by the school. The challenge, as identified by the students in this project's focus groups, is when the definition of those categories is unclear. Some terms are self-explanatory copyright infringement defines itself, as does "illegal." Other terms have legal definitions that one would expect the

Table 7.1 Readability of cyberspeech handbook entries

	Mean	Median	St. Dev.	GL[1] 9–12	GL 13–17	GL 18+
Fog index	16.39	15.31	3.107	2	22	11
Coleman–Liau	14.92	14.9	1.77	3	31	1
Flesch–Kincaid	14.70	14.04	3.03	4	27	4
ARI	14.49	13.71	3.68	8	21	6

[1]"Grade Level" of readability.

school to apply; for example, "obscenity" has a legal definition created by the *Miller v. California*[3] case that provides clarity in application.

What, however, is "harassment" or "discrimination"? Several policies use the term "harmful to minors" or "inappropriate materials" without description about how harm or appropriateness is defined or who gets to identify it. Clarity in definitions remains a consistent issue for offline *and* online speech.

Perhaps more concerning is the presentation of prohibited or punishable online speech. Many of these policies are grounded in the need for the school or district to regulate use of its equipment or network. The introduction to these online policies begins with a statement of the valuable tool that the internet provides to modern education combined with the responsibility of the school to ensure that the resource *it provides* to its students is used effectively and appropriately for the educational process. This makes sense—a school can create regulation to guide and protect the appropriate use of its resources, ranging from the cafeteria to textbooks to the school's wi-fi network. As the policies start to explore types of cyberspeech, however, the conversation drifts from speech that occurs using school equipment or networks to student online speech in general. For example:

> Students shall not send, post, or possess electronic messages that are abusive, obscene, sexually oriented, threatening, harassing, damaging to another's reputation, or illegal, including cyberbullying and "sexting," either on or off school property, if the conduct causes a substantial disruption to the educational environment.[4]

The wording of this example doesn't suggest a limitation to speech created on school equipment or the school networks—the plain reading of it explicitly seems to embrace all student speech that may occur online. This school's student handbook did include an additional step that aligns with lower federal court approaches to online speech by confining its regulation to the *Tinker* standard, or speech that causes a substantial disruption to the educational environment.

Here we can see where the focus group students' concerns about clarity and context can be relevant to handbook language discussing cyberspeech. Policies need to clarify and contextualize not only the categories of speech to which they apply, but also the circumstances that trigger their application. The example cited earlier clarifies that off-campus speech will be regulated if it poses a disruptive effect to the academic environment—this level of context helps students understand when the school is authorized to act.

A more compelling question for schools attempting to address student cyberspeech in their student handbooks is if it should be treated separately from offline speech at all. Speech is speech—there is no separate First Amendment for the Internet. The U.S. Supreme Court has given online speech the same rights and responsibilities as print,[5] refusing to analyze such speech more rigorously or differently because of its platform. Should schools do so?

According to the *Tinker* standard, schools are empowered to regulate student speech when such speech disrupts (or can reasonably be forecast to disrupt) the academic environment. This precedent has been applied to a wide variety of student speech, including when such expression occurs online. Student handbooks would be well served to consider a similar platform-neutral approach to express the rights and responsibilities of the students in their learning communities.

This is not to say that schools should not create rules regarding the use of school technology and networks, and include that clear policy language in student handbooks. These are property issues that can create legal and personal liability concerns. But when schools are trying to explain speech rights and responsibilities to their students through student handbooks, acknowledging the expectation of nondisruptive speech as well the ability to prohibit speech that already lacks First Amendment protection (such as obscenity, true threats, and defamation) does not need differentiation by platform.

Taking a uniform approach to student speech rights and responsibilities in student handbooks may result in a greater benefit to students by reinforcing the general power of responsible speech. If a student handbook separates offline from online speech, it suggests to students that they should treat their expression differently if it is online versus offline. That creates a false expectation of legal and social difference between the two— one that does not bear out in the real world. All speech has a degree of freedom, and all speech has a degree of responsibility. Reinforcing that in student handbooks creates a learning experience that feeds into the larger benefit that free speech presents to the academic environment.

FOUR STEPS TO CLEARER STUDENT SPEECH HANDBOOK ENTRIES

At the end of this exploration comes application: what do we do with this newfound knowledge? The readability analyses, textual reviews, and focus groups do present some recurring themes that schools can use as they craft student handbook language addressing student speech rights and responsibilities.

A first step, which must occur before the "Four steps to clearer student speech handbook entries" can even be discussed, is to ensure schools include an entry on student speech in their student handbooks in the first place. Only 23 of the 45 handbooks for public schools examined in this project included an entry that addressed student speech, and those entries ranged from a scant 26 words to a more descriptive 614. The true first step, then, is to commit to including the discussion in a handbook in the first place.

That can be tough advice to hear. As federal, state, and district mandates continue to require more and more information be included in student handbooks, the idea of fitting even more content in is less attractive. As schools attempt to reduce paper costs and waste while ensuring students are aware of the rules that guide their conduct within their schools, they tend to want to have fewer pages in handbooks, not more.

Remember, however, that student handbooks fill a crucial Fourteenth Amendment role within our public schools—they help ensure that the right to due process is honored and secured. Students need to be able to understand what their free speech rights and responsibilities are within their schools order to use those rights well and wisely. Including an entry on student speech and expression rights that is written in language crafted for the 9- to 12-grade level takes students one step closer to that goal.

The inclusion of a section on speech rights is no guarantee that students will, in fact, know what their rights are. Just because people have access to information about rights and responsibilities does not ensure they will take advantage of such access—for example, a 2015 study revealed more than a third of online users never read terms of use statements for services such as social media or retailing before clicking "I agree." Another 50 % stated that they "sometimes" read the documents, but not necessarily in their entirety. The number one reason for merely browsing documents that outline their rights to privacy, information integrity, and publicity is that "there is no point because you need to 'agree' to sign up, even if you disagree with the content of the terms."[6]

Including information about student expression rights in student handbooks is not a solution to all student speech problems, but it is a start. Once schools make the commitment to including a speech/expression section in student handbooks, this project proposes four steps to clearer, more proactive handbook language.

1. Outline both rights and responsibilities for all forms of expression

Students in the focus groups were disheartened by policies that focused only on what they could *not* do or say. They interpreted this as a lack of support for responsible student speech, and felt it denied them examples of permitted speech that could help them see the rationale for both allowed and disallowed speech. Consider this positive-first example from Washington State:

> The free expression of student opinion is an important part of education in a democratic society. Students' verbal and written expression of opinion on school premises is encouraged so long as it does not substantially disrupt the operation of the school.[7]

This policy acknowledges the presumption of protection before presenting the terms under which student speech could be regulated. If the positive-first approach is ignored and student handbook language on speech instead focuses only what students cannot say or do without punishment, the language undermines the potential value of free speech within the educational environment.

Here, too, schools can embrace emphasizing the platform-neutral approach to speech regulation. Would the statement from the Washington high school listed earlier differ if the speech occurred offline or online? Reinforce that all speech has value, but that students need to understand their responsibilities for all speech as well. Don't train young minds to believe that different rules apply to cyberspeech—rather, help them see that all speech has power to both help and harm, and students must face the benefits or consequences accordingly.

2. Use structure to enhance readability

While readability formulas differ on their approaches toward calculating the grade level needed to fully comprehend text, they universally note that shorter sentences, shorter paragraphs, and active voice lead to greater understanding. These structural elements were very common in the dress codes sections, and likely contributed strongly to their significantly lower readability scores.

Student expression sections can adopt a similar approach as that of dress codes and bring readability more in line with the grades they are meant to serve. A common structure among the dress codes was to present a sentence that introduces a core concept, and then support that statement with a bulleted list of explanations or examples. That approach can work for student speech as well—take, for example, this policy from Pennsylvania:

> Students are expected to use appropriate, constructive language while in school, on school property, on school grounds, or attending school-sponsored activities.
>
> Written or verbal comments or gestures that are obscene, rude, threatening, harassing, or insubordinate in nature shall be construed as forms of inappropriate language. Such inappropriate language will be subject to disciplinary action.
>
> For purposes of student speech, it is regulated here only insofar as it:
>
> - substantially disrupts or interferes with the work of the school or the rights of other students;
> - is lewd, vulgar or profane; or
> - is school-sponsored, i.e., speech that a reasonable observer would view as the school's own speech.[8]

This policy's readability scores fall between 11th and 12th grade. The short, active-voice sentences and bulleted list help maintain an appropriate readability while still conveying clear direction for students.

3. Provide definitions and examples

Focus group students made it clear that they understood the limitations of handbook language. They do not expect lists of allowed or disallowed speech to be all-inclusive or definitive, nor do they expect policies to be written so closely that they address every possible hypothetical scenario. But they do want to have a sense for what is allowed and disallowed, and definitions and examples provide guidance for students to predict how a policy might be applied in a given situation.

Many categories of speech have clear legal definition, such as obscenity or defamation, and others have clear social definition, such as lewdness or profanity. Where students find themselves needing clearer definition is terms like "appropriate" or "disruptive." The inherent vagueness of these terms leaves both student and teacher in limbo, which can result in inconsistent application of policy and a handbook that fails to accurately state student rights.

This policy from an Alabama public high school student handbook provides one approach to definition/examples:

Students may not engage in speech, expression or behavior which:

- Is obscene to minors,
- Is libelous or slanderous,
- Is Indecent, lewd or vulgar,
- Advertises any product or service not permitted to minors by law,
- Injures, harasses, or invades the privacy of other people including, but not limited to, speech or expression which defames any person on the basis of his/her race, sex, color, creed or religion,
- Will either result, or which school administrators reasonably forecast will result, in a material and substantial disruption of the orderly operation of the school and/or school activities.

This list is not exhaustive. School administrators may prohibit any type of speech, dancing, dress, or expression that is inconsistent with school system policy.[9]

This example allows students to get a better sense for actionable types of speech as well as the types of harms the school is trying to prevent through this policy. There is room for improvement—for example, this handbook language does not provide explanation or definition of the "material and substantial disruption"—but, as a whole, this expression entry does create a frame of reference for students to apply to parallel situations.

4. Explain how context is created—and why

Within phrases such as "inappropriate" or "disruptive" are judgment calls on the worthiness of student speech within the academic environment. That environment is not uniform—the classroom is not the cafeteria, hallway, or athletic field. Each of these locations within the academic environment creates different social expectations and norms, which allow for different expectations of speech. Students want to know how that context will be taken into consideration when questions of appropriateness or disruption are examined, and whose judgment will be brought to bear when student-to-student communication is examined.

The question is worthwhile. In a dissent in *Fraser*, Justice John Paul Stevens noted that a student is "probably in a better position to determine whether an audience composed of 600 of his contemporaries would be offended by the use of a four-letter word—or a sexual metaphor—than is a group of judges who are at least two generations and 3000 miles away from the scene of the crime."[10] Teachers remain the best authority on appropriate speech within the classroom, but in other parts of the academic environment, it may be that students have far more accurate insight into the appropriateness of speech among their peers.

The "context" question is not an advocacy to surrender control of disciplinary decisions to student judgment. It merely advocates that when discussing student speech within the student handbook, acknowledging the relevance of student perspectives in establishing the context of the speech goes a long way toward recognizing the roles students have in creating and maintaining the social norms of their relationships with one another.

Runner up: There's no universal approach to student speech language for student handbooks.

In a perfect world, a project like this would generate a template for schools to use to include student speech entries in handbooks. One of this project's key takeaways—that cultural norms are as significant to understanding as sentence structure—makes a one-size-fits-all template untenable. It has to reflect the unique culture of your school, the policies of your district/school board, and the guidance of your state. It has to match the tone and language of your other handbook sections, to read as a comprehensive whole. Perhaps most importantly, it has to be created for your students by you—the educators who know your students best.

Why It Matters

Including an entry on student speech and expression rights within the student handbook helps ensure that students' due process rights are protected. Yet this is only part of the reason why student speech policies—and their clear articulation in student handbooks—is so important.

Free speech has inherent educational value.[11] It allows students to engage with critical thinking and analysis of their world around them as well as themselves. Thomas Emerson wrote that free speech fulfilled four key roles in society: assuring self-fulfillment, advancing knowledge, enabling participation in decision making and creating a more adaptable community.[12] All of these elements apply to the academic environment as well. By freely sharing ideas and opinions, students are able to better self-define and shape their autonomous perspectives on the world. Such sharing also allows them to learn new things and participate in the decisions that shape their world. And through open discussion with peers, teachers, and administrators, they contribute to the adjustments that their learning environments must go through to adapt to a constantly changing society.

Free speech in schools not only contributes to a present benefit, but also a future one. A variety of studies have linked participation in high school media with higher rates of later civic engagement[13]—most recently, the University of Kansas's Piotr Bobkowski showed through nationally representative data that high school journalism participation not only positively correlates to post-high school voting, but that it also moderates an inverse relationship between socioeconomic status and civic engagement.[14]

Student newspapers, as a vehicle of expression, are a little narrower than "student speech," per se, but they are a very tangible representation of speech and expression rights within the academic environment. Students who have the opportunity to engage with the rights and responsibilities of free speech through their student newspapers (which are, admittedly, limited per the U.S. Supreme Court) *are more likely* to continue to use their voice in their communities after graduation, through voting or other civic engagement activities.[15]

Allowing students a degree of clear freedom to express themselves, even to disagree, plants the idea that their opinions have meaning and merit. This can be successfully done within the educational environment without sacrificing the order needed to effectively educate. Doing so provides the needed balance for students to understand how to engage with speech now and in the future—as author Amy Gutmann wrote, "Children must learn not just to behave in accordance with authority but to think critically about authority if they are to live up to the democratic ideal of sharing political sovereignty as citizens."[16]

The right to free speech is an exercise in balance of the unique value of free speech to a democratic society against the potential harms that speech may incur. The U.S. Supreme Court's treatment of student speech in public schools reflects that balance by acknowledging a student's right to free speech as well as the necessity for an orderly and productive learning environment. If one begins to outbalance the other, a constitutional issue arises.

Districts maintain this balance through the creation of policy that protects both the student and the school. Individual schools can extend this protection one step further by adopting clear, grade-appropriate student speech entries in student handbooks. Doing so not only works to ensure that students can understand the expression rules that guide their day-to-day activities in their school environment, but also reinforce the importance of engaging in thoughtful, responsible expression on topics that are important to their lives. It will help remind them that their voices matter—a unique and valuable lesson for us all.

NOTES

1. *See* M.D. Thomson & L. Hoffman-Goetz, "Readability and cultural sensitivity of web-based patient decision aids for cancer screening and treatment: A systematic review," *Medical Informatics & The Internet in Medicine* 32, no. 4 (2007): 263–286. or J.J. Guidry, P. Fagan & V. Walker. "Cultural sensitivity and readability of breast and prostate printed cancer education materials targeting African Americans," *Journal of the National Medical Association* 90, no. 3 (1998): 165–169.
2. Twin Valley School District (Pa.), "TVHS Student Handbook" (2014).
3. 413 U.S. 15 (1973).
4. Bay City High School (Texas). "Bay City Junior High and High School Student Handbook and the Student Code of Conduct" (2014).
5. Reno v. American Civil Liberties Union 521 U.S. 844 (1997).
6. Kimberlee Morrison. "Survey: Many Users Never Read Social Networking Terms of Service Agreements," *SocialTimes/AdWeek.com* (2015).
7. Everett Public Schools (Wash.), "Student Responsibilities & Rights Policies" (2014).
8. Twin Valley School District (Pa.), "TVHS Student Handbook" (2014).
9. Leeds City Schools (Ala). "Student Handbook" (2009).
10. *Bethel* 478 U.S. at 692 (Stevens, J. dissenting).
11. Mary Sue Backus, "OMG! * Missing the Teachable Moment and Undermining the Future of the First Amendment–TISNF! **," *Case Western Reserve Law Review* 60, no. 1 (2009): 200.
12. Thomas I. Emerson, *The System of Freedom of Expression* (New York: Random House, 1970) 6–7.
13. Lonnie Sherrod, Constance Flanagan and James Youniss, "Dimensions of Citizenship and Opportunities for Youth Development: The What, Why, When, Where and Who of Citizenship Development" *Applied Developmental Science* 6, No. 4 (2002): 266.
14. P.S. Bobkowski & P.R. Miller. "Civic implications of secondary school journalism: Associations with voting propensity and community volunteering," *Journalism and Mass Communication Quarterly*, published online before print doi: 10.1177/1077699016628821 (2016).

15. For examples of studies that support this idea, see *Civic Engagement Among High School Journalists* at http://civicsandjournalists.org/category/prior-research/.
16. Amy Gutmann, *Democratic Education* (Princeton, NJ: Princeton University Press, 1999) 51.

REFERENCES

Backus, M. S., "OMG! * Missing the Teachable Moment and Undermining the Future of the First Amendment–TISNF! **," *Case Western Reserve Law Review 60*, no. 1 (2009): 153–204.

Bay City High School (Texas). "Bay City Junior High and High School Student Handbook and the Student Code of Conduct" (2014).

Bethel v. Fraser 478 U.S. 675 (1986).

Bobkowski, P. S., & Miller, P. R., "Civic implications of secondary school journalism: Associations with voting propensity and community volunteering," *Journalism and Mass Communication Quarterly* published online before print doi: 10.1177/1077699016628821 (2016).

Civic Engagement Among High School Journalists, http://civicsandjournalists.org (n.d., last accessed July 5, 2016).

Emerson, T. I., *The System of Freedom of Expression*. New York: Random House, (1970).

Everett Public Schools (Wash.), "Student Responsibilities & Rights Policies" (2014).

Guidry, J. J., Fagan, P., & Walker, V., "Cultural sensitivity and readability of breast and prostate printed cancer education materials targeting African Americans," *Journal of the National Medical Association 90*, no. 3 (1998): 165–169.

Gutmann, A., *Democratic Education*. Princeton, NJ: Princeton University Press, (1999).

Morrison, K. "Survey: Many Users Never Read Social Networking Terms of Service Agreements," *SocialTimes/AdWeek.com* (2015).

Leeds City Schools (Ala). "Student Handbook" (2009).

Miller v. California 413 U.S. 15 (1973).

Reno v. American Civil Liberties Union 521 U.S. 844 (1997).

Sherrod, L., Flanagan, C., & Youniss, J., "Dimensions of Citizenship and Opportunities for Youth Development: The What, Why, When, Where and Who of Citizenship Development," *Applied Developmental Science 6*, no. 4 (2002): 264–272.

Thomson, M. D., & Hoffman-Goetz, L., "Readability and cultural sensitivity of web-based patient decision aids for cancer screening and treatment: A systematic review," *Medical Informatics & The Internet in Medicine 32*, no. 4 (2007): 263–286.

Twin Valley School District (Pa.), "TVHS Student Handbook" (2014).

APPENDICES

APPENDIX 1

State laws requiring the creation and/or distribution of conduct/responsibilities policies (either general rules and policies or specific to conduct such as bullying or harassment)

Alabama	Ala. Code §16-28A-3	"...the State Board of Education shall require each local board of education to develop a written policy on student discipline and behavior and to broadly disseminate them"
Arizona	Ariz. Rev. Stat. § 15-341, 37(c)	"...school officials provide all pupils with a written copy of the rights, protections and support services available to a pupil"
Arkansas	Ark. Code. Ann. § 6-18-502(e)	"Each school district shall develop a procedure for written notification to all parents and students of the district's student discipline policies and for documentation of the receipt of the policies by all parents and students"
Colorado	Colo Rev. Stat. § 22-32-109.1	"...Copies of the code shall be provided to each student upon enrollment at the elementary, middle, and high school levels..."
Iowa	Iowa Code § 280.28 (3)	"...the board and the authorities shall make a copy of the policy available to all school employees, volunteers, students, and parents or guardians..."

(continued)

© The Author(s) 2017
E. Salkin, L. Shenkel, *Student Speech Policy Readability in Public Schools*, DOI 10.1007/978-3-319-44132-0

(continued)

Kansas	Kan. Stat. Ann. § 91-15-1	"The board of education of each unified school district shall adopt policies or rules that govern the conduct of the employees and students of the school district"
Kentucky	Ky. Rev. Stat. Ann. § 158.148.4(e)	"A copy of the code of behavior and discipline adopted by the board of education shall be posted at each school....All school employees and parents, legal guardians, or other persons exercising custodial control or supervision shall be provided copies of the code."
Massachusetts	Mass. Gen. Laws ch. 71, § 37(H)	"The superintendent of every school district shall publish the district's policies pertaining to the conduct of teachers and students."
Oregon	Or. Rev. Stat. § 339.240 (2)	"Every district school board shall adopt and attempt to give the widest possible distribution of copies of reasonable written rules regarding pupil conduct, discipline and rights and procedures pertaining thereto"
Pennsylvania	22 Pa. Code §12.3(c)	"Each governing board shall adopt a code of student conduct that includes policies governing student discipline and a listing of students' rights and responsibilities as outlined in this chapter. This conduct code shall be published and distributed to students and parents or guardians. Copies of the code shall also be available in each school library."
South Carolina	S.C. Code. Ann. § 59-63-140 (D)	"The local school board shall ensure that the school district's policy developed pursuant to this article is included in the school district's publication of the comprehensive rules, procedures, and standards of conduct for schools and in the student's handbook"
Texas	Tex. Educ. Code Ann. § 37.001(a)	"The board of trustees of an independent school district shall, with the advice of its district-level committee established under Subchapter F, Chapter 11, adopt a student code of conduct for the district. The student code of conduct must be posted and prominently displayed at each school campus or made available for review at the office of the campus principal"

(continued)

Vermont	Vt. Stat. Ann. tit. 16, §1161a (a)	"Each public and each approved independent school shall adopt and implement a comprehensive plan for responding to student misbehavior."
Washington	Wash. Admin. Code 392-400-225	"It shall be the responsibility and duty of each school district to adopt, publish, and make available to all students and parents written rules which state with reasonable clarity the types of misconduct for which discipline, suspension, and expulsion may be imposed."
Wisconsin	Wis. Stat. §120.13 (1)(1)	"Make rules for the organization, gradation and government of the schools of the school district, including rules pertaining to conduct and dress of pupils in order to maintain good decorum and a favorable academic atmosphere"

APPENDIX 2

The student handbook sample

Handbooks were located from each randomly selected high school's website. The year of the handbook follows the school's name in parenthesis.

Alabama	George Washington Carver High School (2011–12)
	Homewood High School (2013–14)
	Leeds High School (2009–10)
Arizona	Amphitheater High School (2014–15)
	Horizon High School (2014–15)
	Maricopa High School (2014–15)
Arkansas	Arkadelphia High School (2013–14)
	Hazen High School (2014–15)
	Mount Ida High School (2014–15)
Colorado	Del Norte High School (2014–15)
	Erie High School (2014–15)
	Sierra High School (2013–14)
Iowa	Ballard High School (2014–15)
	Nashua–Plainfield Junior/Senior High School (2014–15)
	South Hardin High School (2014–15)
Kansas	Abilene High School (2014–15)
	Atchison High School (2013–14)
	Sabetha High School (2014–15)
Kentucky	Atherton High School (2013–14)
	Henry Clay High School (2015–16)
	Shelby County High School (2013–14)
Massachusetts	Andover High School (2014–15)
	Middleborough High School (2015–16)
	West Bridgewater Middle/High School (2014–15)
Oregon	Corvallis High School (2014–15)
	Philomath School District (2014–15)
	Toledo Jr/Sr High (2012–13)
Pennsylvania	Central Bucks High School East (2014–15)
	East Forest Junior/Senior High School (2014–15)
	Twin Valley High School (2014–15)
South Carolina	Abbeville high School (2014–15)
	Aynor High School (2014–15)
	Spartanburg High School (2014–15)
Texas	Academy High School (2014–15)
	Bay City High School (2014–15)
	Lampasas High School (2014–15)

(continued)

Vermont	Blue Mountain Union School (2014–15)
	Milton High School (2014–15)
	South Burlington High School (2014–15)
Washington	Cascade High School (2014–15)
	Franklin Pierce High School (2014–15)
	Pomeroy Jr/Sr High School (2014–15)
Wisconsin	Amherst High School (2011–12)
	Central High School (2014–15)
	Palmyra-Eagle High School (2010–11)

APPENDIX 3

Sample student speech policies

Policy 1

Students are entitled to express their personal opinions verbally, symbolically and in writing in a manner consistent with the First Amendment, considering the special nature of the school setting. True threats of violence and language or ideas of such a nature that it is reasonably probable that the expression will cause violent or unlawful behavior are not expression protected by the First Amendment and are not acceptable in the school setting.

Other forms of student expression that are not expression protected by the First Amendment and are not acceptable in the school setting expressions that are: (1) profane, vulgar or obscene; (2) that reference illegal drug use, or that (3) will materially and substantially interfere with the maintenance and operation of the schools, including, but not limited to, the preservation of the educational process. Student expression that constitutes harassment or discrimination based on race, religion, color, national origin or ancestry, sex, gender identity, sexual orientation, age, marital or veteran status, or disability will not be tolerated.

– from Tacoma Public Schools (Wash.), Student Rights, Responsibilities and Regulations (2010).

Policy 2

Students are entitled to express their opinions verbally, symbolically and in writing. Student expression may not contain language or ideas that one could reasonably assume will create hostility, violence or unlawful behavior; be libelous, slanderous, profane, vulgar or obscene; or materially or substantially interfere with the educational process.

– from Bellingham Public Schools (Wash.), Family Handbook and Calendar (2015).

INDEX

© The Author(s) 2017
E. Salkin, L. Shenkel, *Student Speech Policy Readability in Public Schools*, DOI 10.1007/978-3-319-44132-0